The Nuts and Bolts of Deacon Ministry

Alice Cullinan
Keith Dixon

Acknowledgements

Our heartfelt thanks to the pastors and deacons who attended the training sessions that we led for the Greater Cleveland County Baptist Association, Shelby, N.C. over the past ten years. Their faithful attendance at the conferences, along with their kind words of encouragement regarding the helpfulness of what we taught was the catalyst for the writing of this book. Both of us have served alongside many faithful pastors and deacons, and are grateful for the ways that they impacted our lives and influenced the spread of the Gospel.

We also want to thank Deveron Helgeson, faithful Sunday School Teacher and friend, and Jim Cullinan, who served as Chair of Deacons at his church, for their encouragement, helpful comments, and editing suggestions. And special gratitude is expressed to Carolyn Sears, pastor and Co-Founder of Lamplighters Ministries, for her labor of love evidenced in many hours spent editing and offering design ideas and suggestions.

We want to thank our families, too – of course! – for the support and guidance they have shown to us throughout our lives. I (Alice) want especially to express my gratitude to Irene Coalter for introducing me to Jesus, and to Mother and Dad, whose lives helped me develop a servant's heart. I (Keith) am thankful for the support of my family and especially for my Dad, the best example of a deacon/servant that I know.

© **Copyright by LampLighters Ministries, 2016**

LampLighters Ministries
104 Annies Circle
Shelby. N.C. 28152

lamplighters-ministries.org
lamplightersministries@gmail.com

All rights reserved. No part of this publication may be translated, reproduced, or transmitted in any form or by any means, electronic or mechanical, including photocopy, recording, or any informational storage and retrieval system, without permission in writing from the authors, except for brief quotations included in a review of the book.

Bible quotations in this volume are from:

The Holy Bible: New International Version, copyright 1973, 1978, 1984. Used by permission of Zondervan Bible Publishers. All rights reserved.

The Holy Bible: Amplified Version, copyright 1954, 1958, 1964, 1987 by the Lockman Foundation. All rights reserved. Used by permission.

The Holy Bible: The Living Bible, copyright 1971. Used by permission of Tyndale House Publishers, Inc., Carol Stream, Ill. 60188. All rights reserved.

The Holy Bible: The Message, copyright 1993, 1994, 1995, 1996, 2000, 2001, 2002. Used by permission of New Press Publishing Group. All rights reserved.

Printed by: Westmoreland Printers, Shelby, N.C.

TABLE OF CONTENTS

Preface: **How to Use This Book** 11
Introduction 13

Section 1: Being the Servant God Called You To Be

Chapter 1: Understanding the Role of the Deacon 17
   The Origin and Qualifications of Deacon Ministry
   The Spiritual Life of the Deacon
   What is Spirituality?
   A Look at Spirituality in Our Churches
   Examining Your Own Spiritual Maturity
   Leading Others to Spiritual Maturity
   Understanding Hindrances to Spirituality
   Living Above the Downward Pull

Chapter 2: Listening to the Voice of God 39
   How God Spoke to Individuals in the Bible
   Lessons from Bible Characters
   Do I Really Want God to Speak to Me?
   Primary Ways God Speaks to People Today
   The Importance of Hearing God's Voice
   Hindrances to Hearing God's Voice: Satan's Schemes

Chapter 3: Understanding Personality Types and Spiritual Gifts 55
   Personality Types and Their Impact on the Church
   Personality Types: the Myers-Briggs Type Indicator
   Taking a Closer Look at Myself
   Understanding Spiritual Gifts
   Basic Principles About Spiritual Gifts
   Prerequisites For Discovering Your Spiritual Gift(s)
   Discovering Your Spiritual Gift(s)

Chapter 4: Serving in the Power of God 75
   Power as Demonstrated in the Old Testament
   Learning From Peter the Apostle
   Becoming Powerful Servants
   Scriptural Reminders Regarding the Power of God
   Understanding Spiritual Burnout
   Why is Ministry Burnout so Prevalent?
   Avoiding Spiritual Burnout

Section 2: Improving the Spiritual Health of Your Church

Chapter 5: **Assessing the Spiritual Health of Your Church** 97
What Makes a Church Healthy?
The Balance Between Maintenance and Mission
Maintaining a Good Balance
Winning Jesus' Approval
Jesus' Assessment of His Churches
The Challenge

Chapter 6: **Meeting Requirements for Effective Church Ministry** . . . 111
The First Requirement: Building a Strong Foundation
The Second Requirement: Maintaining a Proper Balance
The Third Requirement: Staying on Track

Chapter 7: **Following Jesus, The Head of the Church** 129
Jesus, The Head of the Church, According to Paul
Connected or Disconnected?
Being a Great Commission Church
A Portrait of Great Commission Deacons and Churches
The Heart of the Matter: Recover the Awe
Recovering the Awe

Chapter 8: **Knowing and Doing God's Will** 153
Why it is Difficult to Discern God's Will
Pre-requisites for Knowing the Will of God
God's Will: Lessons from Adam and Eve
How You Can Help Your Church Obey God's Will
The Will of God and Your Life

Section 3: Handling the Administrative Tasks

Chapter 9: Learning Hands-On Ministry Strategies 169
    The Deacon's Role As Minister
    Ministry in Hospital Situations
    Ministry to the Bereaved
    The Ministry of Encouragement
    Ministry to the Elderly
    Developing a Servant's Heart

Chapter 10: Managing Organizational Tasks 183
    Policies and Procedures
    Staff: Calling and Exit Strategies
    Working With Staff, Leaders, and Committees
    Deacon Elections
    Deacon Family Ministry
    Deacons' Meetings
    Deacon Ethics

Chapter 11: Handling Church Conflict 197
    What is Conflict?
    Strategies for Handling Conflict
    How the Early Church Handled Conflict
    Basic Principles About Conflict Resolution

Conclusion 213

Preface: How to Use This Book

Suggestions for *individual* study:

1. As you read, be sure to take time to answer the questions posed, and complete the inventories. These times of reflection will be very beneficial to you.
2. Take time to read each chapter in sequential order. There is a reason that we wrote the chapters in this order. Although the content is helpful in any order that you choose, you will be more likely to gain insight into how best to help your church when your own heart has been touched and challenged first. You may be tempted to read chapters dealing with specific issues that your church presently faces, but those chapters will be more helpful if you have read the book in sequential order.
3. As you read, if something challenges you, stop right then and pray about it.
4. It is always helpful to journal your thoughts, but if you do not want to do that, consider sharing what you are thinking and feeling with at least one other person, preferably someone who has also read the book.
5. This book contains a wealth of information. Don't think you have to master all of it during just one reading! Read and re-read segments of it over a period of time until its truths become deeply imbedded in your heart and life.

Suggestions for *group* study:

The pastor, chair of the deacons, or other leader can:

1. Assign a portion of the material for each deacon to read and be prepared to discuss during a segment of deacons' monthly meetings. Or, you can divide the deacon body into groups, assigning each group a certain topic to discuss during the meeting.
2. Plan a retreat for the discussion of the book. (The pastor or deacon chair should decide how best to present the material.) Deacons should be encouraged to read the book before the retreat, and to complete beforehand whichever inventories the study leaders request.
3. Schedule a monthly deacon training class for new (or all) deacons, which will last 11 months, covering one chapter per month.
4. When issues arise in the church that are addressed in the book, encourage the deacons to read and discuss that material before attempting to address the issue(s) at hand.
5. As you read, realize that certain topics should be studied church-wide (spiritual gifts, personality differences, etc.). Changes to be implemented (constitutional changes, safety issues, etc.) should be addressed church-wide as well. Take time to address these issues in your meetings and with the church as a whole.

You have our permission to duplicate any of the surveys to use with your church members as long as you have purchased a copy of this book and placed the following information on the sheet(s): *From* <u>Nuts and Bolts of Deacon Ministry</u>, *Cullinan and Dixon. Copyright by LampLighters Ministries, 2016. Used by permission.*

Introduction

"Billy?" asked the voice on the phone.

"Yes, this is Billy."

"Billy, this is Chad, deacon chair at church. Did I catch you at a bad time?"

"No, this is fine. What's on your mind, Chad? He couldn't imagine why the deacon chair would call him.

"Billy, I know you and your family were out of town this past Sunday, but I wanted you to know that you have been nominated by the church to serve as deacon for the next three years. Would you be willing to serve if elected by the congregation?"

There was a brief moment of silence. Billy sat down. "I...er...I guess so, Chad. But I don't really know the qualifications or duties of deacons. Is there a way I could find that out before I decide whether to let my name be placed on the ballot?"

Did your own selection as deacon go anything like the above scenario? Did you get a brief or even a lengthy explanation of the expectations of deacons in your church, only to find yourself still overwhelmed with the possibility that God might be calling you to this strategic role? Or have you been elected and are just beginning this exciting journey of ministry? Or you may have been serving as a deacon for many years and still feel like you do not know the extent of God's plan for you and your church.

It is our prayer that this book will be helpful to you in many ways. It is not a pre-packaged agenda everyone must follow, of course. It is a guide to help you understand God's plan for service in His Kingdom, especially for those the church calls to serve as deacons and leaders. We hope the materials will be helpful to everyone who reads the book, to those in other leadership positions in the church and, in fact, to all who want to walk more closely with God.

-Alice Cullinan and Keith Dixon

Section One:

Being The Servant GOD Called You To Be

1. Understanding the Role of the Deacon 17
2. Listening to the Voice of God 39
3. Understanding Personality Types and Spiritual Gifts 55
4. Serving in the Power of God 75

CHAPTER ONE

UNDERSTANDING THE ROLE OF THE DEACON

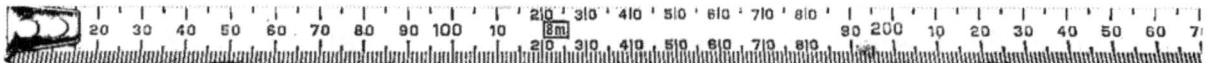

The word *deacon* comes from the Greek work *diakonos*, which means **servant** or **minister**.[1] Most of us think we have a pretty good idea of what a servant role in the church looks like, but it will be helpful to reread the biblical account of the first deacons, as recorded in the Book of Acts.

> *In those days when the number of disciples was increasing, the Hellenistic Jews among them complained against the Hebraic Jews because their widows were being overlooked in the daily distribution of food. So the Twelve gathered all the disciples together and said, "It would not be right for us to neglect the ministry of the word of God in order to wait on tables. Brothers and sisters, choose seven men from among you who are known to be full of the Spirit and wisdom. We will turn this responsibility over to them and will give our attention to prayer and the ministry of the word."*
>
> *This proposal pleased the whole group. They chose Stephen, a man full of faith and of the Holy Spirit; also Philip, Procorus, Nicanor, Timon, Parmenas, and Nicolas from Antioch, a convert to Judaism. They presented these men to the apostles, who prayed and laid their hands on them.*
>
> *So the word of God spread. The number of disciples in Jerusalem increased rapidly, and a large number of priests became obedient to the faith. Now Stephen, a man full of God's grace and power, performed great wonders and signs among the people (New International Version, Acts 6:1-4).*

It is obvious that the main role of the first deacons was to serve. A need arose and they were selected to help meet it. You probably also noticed when you read the passage that the need or problem was voiced as a complaint to the apostles! Sounds familiar, doesn't it? We should notice, also, that the apostles did not try to meet every

---

[1] <u>Holman Bible Dictionary</u>, (Holman Bible Publishers: Nashville, Tennessee, 1991), p. 344.

need or try to solve every problem by themselves. They were wise to select others to serve alongside them. They made a proposal, and the whole group was pleased and the selection took place. This certainly sounds like a good way to do things!

THE ORIGIN AND QUALIFICATIONS OF DEACON MINISTRY

By examining the passage in Acts 6, we will notice that the most important qualifications of the first deacons were stated in this way: **full of the Spirit and wisdom, full of faith and of the Holy Spirit, and full of God's grace and power.** How many people in our congregations would be willing to have their names added to a ballot that listed those qualifications?

There are other qualifications that describe these early deacons, the servants whom the body of believers selected. Acts chapters 6-8 record many of these traits:

1. They knew God's Word and spoke it boldly even when criticized.
2. They were quick to pray and to forgive others, even enemies.
3. They were willing to proclaim Christ, and to minister in significant ways.
4. They were receptive to the Spirit's leading, even when it seemed foolish.
5. They had concern for all and were willing to reach/teach one at a time.
6. They were willing to leave their comfort to reach non-believers.

Do you and the other deacons in your church exhibit these traits?
Where and how can you develop or improve?

The Spiritual Life of the Deacon

He was one of our senior citizens, a church member for many years. Whenever the doors of the church were open, you could expect to see him and his wife there. One Sunday morning, during the invitation hymn, he walked down the church aisle to share that he was accepting Jesus as his personal Savior. The pastor explained to the congregation the struggle this long-time member had recently shared with him, and how he had discovered that he had never really known the Lord personally. All of his spirituality had been second-hand or mere religiosity.

Within a few weeks, another church member, a father of teenage children, also accepted Jesus as his Lord and Savior, although he had grown up in the church and had been active in Bible study for many years. He, too, had come to realize that his faith was not his own, and although he knew many Bible facts, he had missed the most important thing of all: a personal relationship with Jesus Christ.

Unfortunately these stories are not isolated or unique. They happen repeatedly in many of our churches, regardless of denominational affiliation. When I (Alice) was a seminary student, the pastor at the church I attended shared with the congregation that the Lord showed him that he had not really been born again. What a shock to the entire congregation!

How could this happen? How can people who have been in church for most of their lives (some even serving in full-time ministry) miss the most important part of the message that the church proclaims? Who is at fault? What can be done to solve the problem? Have churches created the problem, or have they simply not dealt with the reality that is already there? What is spirituality, anyway? How is it fostered and nurtured? How can we, as church leaders, deal with this important issue?

This is a subject dear to my heart (Alice). My entire family and I were in this very condition for a long time. We were church members and active leaders, but somehow we hadn't realized our need to know Jesus personally, to invite Him into our hearts to be Savior and Lord.

WHAT IS SPIRITUALITY?

There are many ways to define *spirituality* and it will be helpful to examine some definitions in order to help us come to a proper understanding of our own spiritual condition. In his book, Spiritual Awakening: A Guide to Spiritual Life in Congregations, John Ackerman[2] writes:

"Christian spirituality is a specific quality of relationship: loving God, neighbor, and self, and receiving love and grace. Perhaps the fullest expression of Christian spirituality in the New Testament is in Paul's prayer that the Ephesians be *strengthened in your inner being with power through the Spirit, and that Christ may dwell in your hearts through faith, as you are being rooted and grounded in love...and that you know the love of Christ that surpasses knowledge, so that you may be filled with all the fullness of God* (Eph. 3:16-19)." Ackerman goes on to say that "spirituality is the heart attitude behind formal belief and practice."

Webster's dictionary defines *spirituality* as "the state of being concerned with religious matters."[3] Most of us realize that this definition does not adequately deal with *Christian* spirituality. We feel that Christian growth/maturity should be a major goal for all believers. We agree with Ackerman: *spirituality has to do with the quality of our relationship with God.*

For some reason, or for different reasons, it is easy for church members to substitute *vital relationship WITH God* with *activity in the church FOR God*. Becoming acquainted with the church's teachings ABOUT God replaces the individual's experiential knowledge OF God. DOING replaces BEING. WORK replaces WORSHIP. Holiness is a foreign concept to many. Meditation and time for reflection are relegated to those *special saints* who are called by God to be different from most of us. The clergy are viewed as the men and women of prayer and Bible knowledge who impart a word from the Lord to the flock each week. Laypersons often view themselves as second class Christians who cannot attain to the level of spiritual maturity they expect from their paid staff and foreign missionaries. Some expect the 'spiritual people' to give them spiritual food each week when they gather for the morning service. Unfortunately, many also believe that their spiritual responsibility for the week has been satisfied if they attend Sunday School and worship.

---

[2] John Ackerman, Spiritual Awakening: A Guide to Spiritual Life in Congregations (New York: Alban Institute, 1994), x-xi.
[3] Merriam-Webster Dictionary (http://www.merriam-webster.com)

How can we correct these erroneous concepts? Helping someone grow in his or her relationship with God is a process by which the person is taught and/or learns how to allow God's Spirit to be in control of his/her life. God has given us the disciplines of the spiritual life as a means to grow in grace. Bible study, prayer, fasting, worship, silence and witness are just some of the ways God uses to help transform us into the image of His Son. It is up to us to make the effort, to take the time necessary to use those disciplines that connect us with God and His work. For deacons and other church leaders, this is an absolute necessity! Spiritual growth and transformation cannot occur without the spiritual disciplines. It is not something God pours down over our heads. Neither does it occur automatically along with our physical aging. God has ordained these disciplines as the means by which we place ourselves before Him. The spiritual disciplines are also the means by which He works in our hearts to bless and transform us. Since *all believers* are meant to practice the disciplines, what are the ramifications if our leaders neglect them?

A Look at Spirituality in Our Churches

Why don't we see a deeper spirituality in those who have been church members for many years? Statistics reveal that approximately 20% of a church's members do 80% of the work and the giving. Why is that? Why are church-goers (leaders or not) often just as unspiritual in their interactions and ethics as the unchurched? How can people belong to churches and yet display little or no spiritual fruit? How can a church member not have a basic knowledge of God or know of the need to have a personal relationship with Him? What is wrong? Who is at fault? What can be done?

We cannot possibly discover every reason for the lack of spiritual maturity in our churches. We *can*, however, speculate and discuss ideas for bringing us back to a proper emphasis on the necessity of a personal relationship with God. As a deacon in your church, this is one of the most important challenges you face.

Do any of these factors contribute to a lack of spiritual maturity in your congregation?

1. The division between clergy and laity -
Laypeople tend to excuse themselves from the responsibility of personal spiritual growth. Laypersons expect the clergy to be spiritual and to impart wisdom and blessing  to them. Perhaps the clergy has mistakenly accepted this role, or perhaps they want or feel a need to be a step ahead of everyone else spiritually. It may be that they enjoy being placed on a pedestal.

2. The church's shift towards secularism -
At one time, the church was the center of community life, and a highly respected institution. Members were fiercely loyal to their denomination and their local church, and clergy were revered as the voice of authority on ethical standards. There has been a shift towards secularism, which brings increased temptation to sin and greater ease of access to ungodliness readily available via television, the internet, and other media. Today, spiritual maturity is almost a foreign concept. Those who pursue a closer walk with the Lord seem to be respected, but more often they are considered a bit peculiar. Nominal Christianity is the norm, while spiritual maturity is the *strange behavior of a certain few oddballs.*

3. The decreasing role of parents in teaching their children how to walk with God -
Perhaps the church took over this role when parents ceased to fulfill that obligation. It has been suggested that the church is only one generation away from paganism, because of the failure to teach our children about God. That danger has always been present, but we may be the ones who will see it become a reality. Even if that generation is already here, the tide can be turned if a few people will determine to make changes in their own lives, and then in their churches.

4. The teaching and preaching of a cheap Christianity -

Cheap Christianity makes no demands on church members - other than giving, of course! "Come join our nice fellowship!" is certainly more appealing than "Come and give your entire life to God." Perhaps the number of true believers (members of the household of God through regeneration) has been surpassed by the number of unregenerate members. Today's preaching and teaching often leave out the challenges of Christianity and the necessity of the spiritual disciplines. When people attempt to live the Christian life in their own strength, they fail. Failure tempts them to drop out of church or become inactive pew-warmers. They have heard about the ethical standards and demands of the Christian life, but have no idea how to live them out in their own lives. So they leave the church. Or they may stay physically, but leave emotionally and spiritually, because the Christian life is just too frustrating for them.

5. Tradition has become the teacher, while few ask life's hard questions -

If our ancestors in the faith practiced church in a certain way, we think it must be biblical, so we feel obligated to do exactly what they did - in the same way and at the same time. Any attempt to change programs or worship is often considered radical and unacceptable. New ways of worship or prayer are often too uncomfortable, and for some it borders on heresy. Some churches experience inter-generational conflict when the younger generation doesn't care how church was done in the past - they want to experience God for themselves. An older generation may make the mistake of criticizing a younger generation, calling them rebels, rather than teaching and guiding them. The present generation could actually breathe a breath of fresh air into dead churches, if allowed to do so. Without the anchor of Biblical truth and the wisdom of the ages, however, it is likely they will continue to develop their own style of worship and spirituality, emphasizing the emotional aspect of worshipping God.

Some years ago, the youth of my (Alice) church attended a summer Bible Conference. During the first worship service following their return, one of the young men spoke a loud "Amen!" during the sermon. The pastor stopped preaching and remarked that the youth had just returned from summer camp and were "more enthusiastic than usual." Whether he meant it or not, it sounded critical, as if youthful enthusiasm for the Lord should be overlooked until the boy got it out of his system! What a way to stifle someone's praise of the Lord!

EXAMINING YOUR OWN SPIRITUAL MATURITY

People yearn for and sometimes find what people experienced during the Great Awakening: a vital personal relationship with the living God. People do not change into spiritual persons automatically upon becoming a Christian. It is a process of  transformation. Spiritual growth does not automatically happen by attending religious services. Leaders must help people understand that we do not become more spiritual by trying harder, but by trusting more. And we only learn to trust more as we begin to allow God to change us. We should not focus on serving others, but on loving and serving God, who then will serve others *through* us. We don't change ourselves in order to become more spiritual; we are changed as we become more spiritual. Spirituality is *who we are* and *who we are becoming*, NOT *what we are doing* and *what we are learning*. The Apostle Paul clearly emphasized that God expects us to live pure lives in a secular, even pagan society: *to live godly lives in a godless world.*

Once, at a conference for professors in Christian schools who teach spiritual formation and guide ministry interns, the speaker shared an interesting concept. Many, he said, have questions they want to ask God when they get to heaven, but I believe God will ask us something when we arrive. I believe He will ask, **"Why didn't you let me bless you more?"** Perhaps that's the crux of spirituality: learning how to let God bless us more, so we can be a blessing to Him and to others.

Deacons are elected by the church to serve as spiritual leaders, not its board of directors or money managers. They must care about their own *and* the congregation's spiritual growth. Their focus should be, "How can we help others know God better and serve Him more faithfully?" To help others, we must first examine our own lives.

Prayerfully meditate upon the following questions:

1. Who am I spiritually? Have I come to understand and deal with my own relationship with God or lack thereof?
2. Have I come to the realization that my own experiences and education may have blinded me to true spiritual maturity?
3. In my own walk with God, am I comfortable where I am, or am I always seeking to know God better?
4. Is my relationship with God contagious and obvious to others?
5. Have I settled into pious, self-righteous religiosity because I'm a deacon?
6. Do I compare my own spiritual life to others, or do I seek to see how God views my relationship with Him?

7. How faithful am I in studying my Bible, praying and worshipping?
8. Am I a faithful steward of my time, talents, and money?
9. How faithful am I to share my faith with non-Christians?
10. How seriously do I deal with my sins and weaknesses?

How did you do? Are you willing to work on areas where you are lacking? Those called to help others grow in their walk with God must first learn to grow themselves. Until we practice what we preach and teach, we cannot expect others to change. May we always examine ourselves first before we design programs to help others grow in faith.

LEADING OTHERS TO SPIRITUAL MATURITY

Once we have identified where we are in our own lives and where our churches are weak, we can set *specific goals* to deal with problem areas. Simply wishing that we were more spiritual is not a prescription for success. It will be helpful to form a small group of mature believers to study the topic of Christian growth and to set goals. Those goals should be *specific, attainable, observable,* and have reasonable *time limits.* After the goals are set, they should be *presented to the congregation* for study and approval. It is important that the goals be accepted by as wide a constituency as possible. This process will take a long time and must be evaluated periodically.

The next step in the process is to *develop ways to meet the goals.* This is an enormous, but necessary task. It is not necessary to have all components in place before you implement any of it. Small, successful steps will ensure progress in more difficult areas. As progress is made, the study group

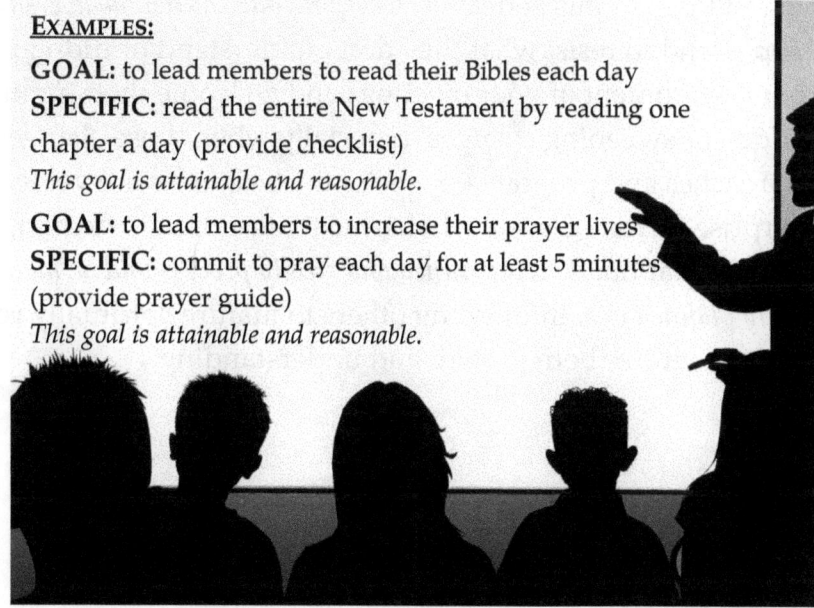

EXAMPLES:
GOAL: to lead members to read their Bibles each day
SPECIFIC: read the entire New Testament by reading one chapter a day (provide checklist)
This goal is attainable and reasonable.

GOAL: to lead members to increase their prayer lives
SPECIFIC: commit to pray each day for at least 5 minutes (provide prayer guide)
This goal is attainable and reasonable.

should *evaluate* how well each aspect of the plan worked, and whether goals were met. *Tweaking the plan*, adding components and dropping others, will be an on-going process.

Clarifying the Issue

How spiritual is your church? How do you judge spirituality? How do you measure who is progressing spiritually and who is not? Recently, in a New Year's sermon, a pastor challenged his flock to go deeper with the Lord that year. He suggested that  someone who only goes to morning worship might consider going one notch deeper by starting to attend a Bible study. Someone who attends only on Sunday mornings might go deeper by starting to attend Sunday night services. Someone who attends every worship service might go deeper by attending the outreach meetings and visiting prospects. These are noble goals, but is this what "spirituality" or "going deeper" really means - to attend more services or go on visitation? It sounds like that pastor thinks so! If we asked him to define spirituality, he probably would NOT describe it as "attending more meetings," yet - intentionally or not - that seemed to be his suggestion to the congregation. Those who teach or preach should examine their own understanding of spiritual maturity. We do not want to confuse the definition/goal with the means for attaining it. We must clearly communicate *and* practice what we actually believe.

As we seek to grow in our faith and to help others do the same, we must remember that change is difficult, and objective self-evaluation is almost impossible. One of the biggest tasks in this endeavor is *keeping our church members both informed and challenged.* People tend to resist what they don't understand or didn't plan, so keep them informed about the content of your meetings and welcome their input. Guard against making sudden or sweeping changes, especially when those changes involve traditional approaches and programs. Some of the best ideas are vetoed simply because of the "surprise factor." Decide what is most important to do first, then carefully plan its implementation. *A well-planned and steady process will be more successful than a hurried and poorly planned one.* Influencing others to mature spiritually requires time and patience; change requires both growth and understanding.

Things to Keep in Mind

One key thing to remember when planning for spiritual growth is that everyone is at a different place on the journey. One size does not fit all. One faith development program  will not suit all church members, nor will one approach to worship benefit everyone. *Variety is essential* in order to help a variety of people, because people simply do not all see things the same way! One way to ensure variety is to put together a planning committee comprised of people of different ages, genders, and personality types. Extroverts' plans will appeal to extroverts; introverts' plans will appeal to introverts. Thinkers will help you be logical; feelers will help you keep in touch with the needs and feelings of others. (You'll learn more about personality types in Chapter Three.) The more *varied the people on your planning committee*, the more likely your plans will succeed with the broad variety of people in your church.

You may want to ask the pastor to address the topic of spiritual growth and maturity by preaching a sermon series and providing additional teaching. You may want to plan some weekend retreats to familiarize people with different worship styles. People will benefit when they learn both how to think about God and how to express their love to Him.

Learning how to share our stories, including victories, struggles, and defeats, is vital to spiritual growth. After Saul of Tarsus encountered Jesus and committed his life to Him, he often told his faith story to any who would listen. He used his own experience to challenge and inspire others as well as to validate his message. One warning here: the work of discovering and understanding your own faith story is hard work. People may tend to imitate others' stories rather than dig deeply inside themselves. Learning to share our faith stories requires patience, encouragement, and guidance.

One could describe the Christian journey as a mountain trail, spiraling upward to heaven. As it ascends, the path winds around and around so that parts of the trail intersect, providing places where pilgrims traveling on different sections of the trail can meet and find fellowship, encouragement, and strength for the journey. One who is further along the way may share what pitfalls or blessings lie ahead, helping to equip others for success on the journey.

It is a great privilege to help fellow believers understand this life as a pilgrimage to glory. We are pilgrims who need the support of other travelers, whose joy it is to invite others to join the procession. Unfortunately, such support among Christians is often lacking. We have fallen into the competition trap. We are sometimes driven to get ahead of others or to out-perform them. We have forgotten (or never learned) the importance of Christian community.

A few summers ago, a qualifying ride for an upcoming bicycle race was held in our small university town. When I (Alice) learned that the cyclists would pass within 200 feet of my house, I took a lawn chair over to my next-door neighbor's yard, and waited with anticipation. It was thrilling to see the riders zoom past me. I noticed, however, that the cyclists were dividing into smaller clusters. The fastest riders took the lead, while others dropped back in the pack. My neighbor shared that sometimes team members lag behind deliberately to help another teammate get ahead of the pack. The distance between the groups of riders was even greater during the final lap. When I thought the race had concluded, I gathered my things to go, but I heard someone crying. I looked up to see a single rider, a woman who was several laps behind all of the others. She obviously was struggling to finish the race. I couldn't help but admire her bravery and determination of spirit as she pushed to complete the race. It would have been much easier to quit.

In many ways, spiritual growth is like that race. It seems there are more spectators than participants. Of those who do enter the race, some work to get ahead, some make sacrifices, some give up hope, and some never quit trying. But all who enter are heading for the prize, eternal life with Christ in Heaven.

You are a spiritual leader in your church – one of the most important races of your life. The goal to hear Jesus say, "Well done, my good and faithful servant," should be what drives your service. We encourage you to take seriously this challenge to go deeper in your relationship with God. We hope you will grow into deeper love for God and others and into diligent and fulfilling service. When you have made the commitment to serve Him to the best of your ability, take advantage of every opportunity to lead others to join you on the journey. Be determined and committed to making sure you and your brothers and sisters in Christ *run to win the prize of the high calling of God in Christ Jesus (Phil 3:14)*.

UNDERSTANDING HINDRANCES TO SPIRITUALITY

When God created humans, He gave them free will. The Creator freely bestowed upon His prize creation the great blessing of fellowship with Himself. He also made it clear to

Adam and Eve that they must stay away from one tree in the middle of the garden - the Tree of the Knowledge of Good and Evil, the fruit of which provided the ability to distinguish right from wrong. Have you ever wondered why God made this prohibition? The tree of the "knowledge of good and evil" represented the opportunity to decide right from wrong *for themselves,* independently of God's advice or authority.

Adam and Eve faced the temptation that confronts us still: to be just as smart as God and free to run our lives as we please. Our intellects are hardly a threat to God, but aren't we still sometimes enamored with our own wisdom? Some Biblical scholars have lost their way, letting go of the anchor of faith in search of knowledge. Sadly, when these wanderers become teachers, their followers often find themselves in places of confusion and doubt instead of certainty and faith.

We are familiar with the rest of Adam and Eve's story. God warned them that they would "surely die" if they ate from the forbidden tree. The humans ate from the tree anyway, but they didn't instantly fall down dead. At first, it looks as if the devil was right when he said, "You will not surely die." But didn't they die? Didn't their loving, close relationship with God end abruptly? They were cast out of the Garden forever, no longer free to walk in sweet fellowship with their Creator. The death principle and process had indeed entered their souls.

Thankfully, our God is a God of love. He was not satisfied to leave His beloved creatures in that state of isolation. In His mercy and grace, He gave His only begotten Son in order to redeem His children back to Himself. We are the recipients of that love. If we have acknowledged our sinfulness and received Jesus as our Savior, then we have been born from above by the Spirit of God. We now have fellowship with God and can be assured that we will live with Him forever.

Many of us, however, have failed to realize that we still possess the Adamic nature, that part of us that constantly rebels against the decrees and supremacy of a loving God. The old nature within us has not yet died. It is very much alive and wants to live life its own way, free of God. The old nature constantly declares, "I am in charge! I make the decisions around here, so don't interfere, because I am the king/queen of this hill (or church or world)." The Adamic nature, the old man of flesh, is alive and well in each of us! The Spirit of God, on the other hand, constantly reminds us of what the Father says: "I love you. I redeemed you from sin when I gave my Son to die in your place. I will come and live within your heart by the power of my Spirit, for that is the only way you can overcome your old nature." Unfortunately, we often believe that we can change the old nature into something God will accept. Remember the following truths. The old nature *cannot* be transformed! The old nature will *never* grow spiritually. The old nature is truly *worthy of death*. It will never get better and it will never change, except to grow more corrupt.

> *You were taught, with regard to your former way of life, to put off your old self,* **which is being corrupted by its deceitful desires** *(Eph 4:22).*

Remember the Cross. It teaches us that God has judged the Adamic nature, and it has been condemned to die. We know that Jesus died *for our sins*, but He also died *in our place*. In God's eyes, our old nature was nailed to the cross with Jesus. That which is of the flesh is flesh; it is unacceptable to a holy God. When we came to faith in Jesus, we experienced new birth - *spiritual birth* - and that which is of the Spirit is spirit, as Jesus reminded His disciples.

> *Very truly I tell you, no one can enter the kingdom of God unless they are born of water and the Spirit.* **Flesh gives birth to flesh, but the Spirit gives birth to spirit.** *You should not be surprised at my saying, "You must be born again." The wind blows wherever it pleases. You hear its sound, but you cannot tell where it comes from or where it is going. So it is with everyone born of the Spirit (Jn 3:4-8).*

REMEMBER THESE TRUTHS:
The old nature *cannot* be transformed!

The old nature will *never* grow spiritually.

The old nature is truly *worthy of death*.

It will never get better and it will never change, except to grow more corrupt.

The Two Gorillas

An analogy of two gorillas can help us understand the two natures within us. Some years ago, I (Alice) was invited to lead a conference for student ministry team leaders at  the university where I taught. When I began to explain the old and new natures that are in Christians, I found myself struggling to get across to them just how much trouble the old nature can cause. I was trying to explain how the old nature often tries to "stay alive" by manifesting religious traits, when out of my mouth came an illustration I had never heard or used before. "A gorilla dressed in a pink tutu is *still* a gorilla!" We had a good laugh, but it is a good description of the old nature and the trouble it causes!

We can plainly see the old natures exhibited in some of the New Testament religious leaders. They were dressed up in their religious garb, yet they could be extremely mean. Highly concerned with ceremonial cleanliness, yet quite eager to kill Jesus, they came up with a solution that wouldn't disqualify their participation in the Passover Feast – kill Jesus and get him buried before Passover began. Today, that would be like a group of deacons dressed in their Sunday best, beating someone to death on the church steps, and then hurrying inside to pass out the bread and juice at the Lord's Supper!

Yes, we have two natures living in us; it's easy to get them confused. Efforts to live the spiritual life in the power of the flesh (the old nature) only bring frustration. Yet we see this picture so often in our churches today: a group of old natures fighting for control of the hill! No matter how hard we might try, my old nature and your old nature are never going to get along!

Recently, I watched a story about the life of a well-known actress. In an interview, she was asked how she felt about playing the part of an evil woman in one of her recent movies. She replied, "We all have a dark side, you know." She spoke an important fact, but apparently was willing to accept the reality of what seems unchangeable. Often, we see this reality of evil dwelling inside of us, but we don't know what to do, either! We do have a dark side, the old nature (or gorilla) that perhaps only our families ever see. Behaviors and attitudes lurk in our dark side that even our families don't know about. That "dark side" is the old nature that God says is worthy of death.

A gorilla in a pink tutu is still a gorilla!

LIVING ABOVE THE DOWNWARD PULL

Without an understanding of the old and new natures, our experience of God's salvation is seriously short-changed. We may find great comfort in the doctrine "once saved, always saved," but maybe we don't realize that our salvation involves much more than the life we will experience some day in heaven. God desires that we commit our lives to Him NOW and that we live in joyful obedience to Him NOW, while we are still living on earth. Too many believe that if we simply keep a few rules and are baptized, that settles it until we die. Some who **profess** to know Jesus just don't seem to **possess** Jesus. There is a big difference in knowing **about** Jesus and having a personal, intimate relationship **with** Jesus. What we must realize is that God wants to save us from the power of the old nature NOW. For many, this aspect of salvation is a foreign concept.

Let's take a closer look at what happens in our hearts as this battle rages inside of us. It is the battle between the old nature and the new nature. Even the apostle Paul, perhaps one of the greatest Christians of the early church, was burdened by this internal struggle. He wrote:

> *I do not understand what I do. For what I want to do I do not do, but what I hate I do. And if I do what I do not want to do, I agree that the law is good. As it is, it is no longer I myself who do it, but it is sin living in me. For I know that good itself does not dwell in me, that is, in my sinful nature. For I have the desire to do what is good, but I cannot carry it out. For I do not do the good I want to do, but the evil I do not want to do—this I keep on doing. Now if I do what I do not want to do, it is no longer I who do it, but it is sin living in me that does it. So I find this law at work: Although I want to do good, evil is right there with me (Rom 7:15-21).*

How do we know which of our two natures is in control? Thankfully, one of the Holy Spirit's roles is to shine His light to reveal what is in our hearts. One major way He does this is through God's Word. We sometimes avoid spiritual inventories and the study of God's Word because we are afraid of what we might learn about ourselves.

Abuse prevention programs train parents how to keep their children safe. They advise parents to teach children to *"Say no, run away and tell an adult when you see a stranger."* This is good advice for us, too. Whenever you see the traits of the old nature crop up in your life, tell it *no,* run away from the sin or temptation and yield to the control of the Holy Spirit.

Psychologists tell us it takes thirty days to develop a habit. Learning how to say *no* to the self and *yes* to the Spirit must become a permanent habit in our lives. Yet, there is a strange phenomenon that happens every night. Sometime, between sleeping and waking, we go back to "default." Just as a computer returns to its default settings when it restarts, so our minds reset when we sleep. When we wake up, the *default settings* are back in place: the self on the throne again! That's why, as early as possible each day, we should make the willful choice to follow Christ, saying *no* to any control by the old nature and submitting ourselves to the Lordship of Christ. We must also ask the Spirit to show us when we try to retake control of our lives. If we make these commitments a daily routine, we will be empowered by the Spirit to live the abundant Christian life.

A Closer Look

Most of us know when we are being tempted to sin, but are we wise to the many ways the flesh (old nature) shows up in our lives? Some of them just seem normal to us. Consider the following works of the flesh that crop up frequently in us.

Circle the ones you have seen in your own life in the past week:

Mind: Love of human praise   Pessimism   Resentment   Selfish ambition   Stubbornness   Egotism   Confusion   Impure thoughts   Judging others   Prayerlessness   Revenge   Disobedience   Troubled   Irritable   Stressed   Unforgiving   Selfishness   Doubt   Unthankful   Worry   Pride

Eyes: Lust   Envy   Greed   Wandering

Ears: Listening to gossip   Attuned to criticism   Closed to spiritual truths

Mouth/Tongue: Criticism of others   Profanity   Boasting   Foolish joking   Rudeness   Lying   Quarreling   Devoid of praise   Grumbling   Hypocrisy   Godless chatter   Complaining   Slander   Dirty jokes   Harshness   Talking too much   Insincere   Dishonest

Heart: Discouraged   Depressed   Full of hatred   Angry   Lonely   Touchy   Hostile   Little enthusiasm   Arrogant   Temper (short fuse)   Unloving   Lazy   Uncompassionate   Impatient   Negative attitude   Worried   Fearful   Guilt   Shame   Anxious   Tense   Nervous   Bitter   Disgusted   Apathetic   Deceitful   Rebellious

(Note: This is just a sample! Ask the Spirit to reveal others to you.)

Remember, the moment you notice the flesh at work in yourself, repent immediately and ask for God's forgiveness. Tell Him you want nothing to do with the old nature or its attempts to control you. Don't try to control the old nature yourself - you can't. Your part is to say *no* to the flesh; that's what it means to deny yourself. Resist the flesh by submitting to the strength of the indwelling Spirit.

There will be times when you will have to literally *run away*. Men, for example, are repeatedly tempted to lust. Some were subjected to pornography as boys, and now its hold on their minds seems almost impossible to break. In order to resist such temptation, you must understand that often our strength is not enough. We must always resist temptation by saying *no*, but sometimes we must physically get away from the source of the pull to do wrong. Some men may never again be able to sit at a computer, with its easy access to pornography, without having in place the necessary safeguards against lust's entrapment. They will have to physically avoid certain sections of bookstores where sexually explicit magazines are readily available. Women, by the way, are not free from this kind of temptation. Females are more prone to become addicted to romance novels or TV soap operas, which they consider an acceptable form of controlled lust.

How can we win these battles between the old and new natures? How can we be empowered to live and walk in the Spirit, instead of being controlled by Satan and the flesh? It is a matter of choice: whom will you obey? To whom will you give control of your life? Consider this scenario: you're in a hurry and are standing in a checkout line when the clerk calls for a price check or the register jams. You hear grumbling from the person behind you. How does your old nature respond? Do you have a choice? Yes! You choose which nature will be in control. You can allow the Spirit to produce patience and kindness in you, or you can let the flesh produce impatience and unkindness. You choose. Learning how to make the right choices is the first step toward true spirituality.

We have all heard about some act of violence resulting from road rage, an emotional response that happens when one driver deems the actions of another driver to be unacceptable. The real problem is that the angry driver feels he/she has lost control of a situation or has been slighted or even attacked in some way. In situations like this, the old nature will usually respond with anger, determined to regain its control of the highway. When the old nature is in control of us, we can experience extreme anger with anyone who gets in our way!

Understanding the Old Nature

Perhaps the most devious strategy of the old nature is its *religious disguise*. Jesus had nothing good to say about religious disguises! The Pharisees considered themselves to  be the most religious persons alive. They prayed, they fasted, they gave exactly the amount of alms required "for righteousness," and they studied the Scriptures incessantly. On the outside, they were pictures of religious perfection, but on the inside they were rotten! Their flesh was religious, but they did not possess the Spirit, which meant their religious practices were an abomination to God. It will benefit us to ask the Lord to show us how many ways our old nature disguises itself as "Christian" in order to make itself seem impressive. May our Lord in His grace give us eyes to see, a heart to repent, and spiritual legs to run the other way from the schemes of the old nature!

Another way the old nature tries to fool us is through its *rationalizations*. It criticizes others, but calls it discernment. It condemns others, but calls it righteous indignation. It judges others, but calls it insight. It rationalizes its own weaknesses away by calling them inherited flaws. It feels pain and hurt, but justifies it in order to keep from repenting of the bitterness, anger, and unforgiveness.

We must remember that original sin came from the desire to make decisions in life without consulting God. These days, we sometimes call this tendency "having control issues," a phrase we've learned to laugh at because it seems like an acceptable way to admit we're stubborn! The reality, however, is that it is always the old nature that wants control, which is always sin in God's eyes. We develop control issues when *someone else* is not doing what *we* want them to do. That uncooperative action really rubs the king of the hill the wrong way!

What can we do when our internal king or queen shows up? Have you learned to say *no* to the flesh, to run the other way from what it wants, and run to the Spirit? Are you praying something like, *There I go again, Lord. Forgive and cleanse me and take back the control I just stole from you*?

There are probably a thousand tricks up the old nature's sleeve! Some are pretty obvious, but others are not. A good way to discover whether our behavior is coming out of the old nature or the new nature is to test our behavior by the fruit of the Spirit. *Love, joy, peace, longsuffering, gentleness, goodness, faithfulness, meekness and self-control (Gal 5:22-23)* - that is the standard by which the new nature lives. The old nature will try to copy some of these virtues, but genuine fruit is verifiable because it is stamped with the character of the Holy Spirit.

There's a saying, "be careful what you ask for - you might get it!" When you ask the Spirit to shine the searchlight on your heart to reveal the old nature - beware! Be ready! He will do it! Be encouraged, because when we "walk in the light as He is in the light," He will purify us from these tendencies and sins, and we will enjoy fellowship with the Lord. If we confess, He cleanses thoroughly (1 Jn 1:9-11).

Paul said that he gloried in the cross alone. He realized that he had a strong old nature that was religious. He had been trained in the way of the Pharisees; he was zealous to the point of persecuting and killing Christians before he met the Lord. He realized that in his old nature he could still be very religious and persuasive, but he also knew that in his flesh "dwelt no good thing" (Rom 7:18). He learned that, in this life, he lived under the bondage of a strong old nature, and that his only hope was to glory in the cross and welcome his own death to self. He learned the secret of trusting in God rather than in himself. More than once, Paul said *I came to you in weakness and fear, and with much trembling. My message and my preaching were not with wise and persuasive words, but with a demonstration of the Spirit's power, so that your faith might not rest on men's wisdom, but on God's power (1 Cor 2:4).*

Are you able to identify when your old nature is in control in your religious life? Have you learned how to tell what thoughts and behaviors come from which nature? Study God's Word daily. The Spirit rejoices in teaching a willing heart.

Opening Our Hearts to God

The scriptures show us the difference between the natural and the spiritual (Heb. 4:12). The Spirit uses the scriptures to judge and analyze the motives of the heart. Study the word of God daily, asking to be searched: "Lord, only you can reveal what comes out of the old or new nature. Help me to see and deal with these things." The Spirit reveals sins and the flesh, not to condemn us, but to free us from its control. If you feel guilty,

ashamed, or worthless, realize that such conviction did not come from God's Holy Spirit, but from Satan or your own old nature. God convicts with a clean, clear cut – not to condemn, but to liberate! He searches us, not to shame us, but to show us the spiritual strength we need. He wants us to confess our sins, allowing Him to cleanse us and fill us with His power.

A friend once made an unfortunate mistake when she purchased some tropical fish without learning the "natures" of each. One of the smaller fish ate all the others! ll know of Christian leaders who have disgraced the name of Christ by falling into sexual sin. What happened? The old nature won out. The old nature and our archenemy Satan entice us to sin in order to destroy our lives and reputations. He wants to hurt us and others, and especially God!

When churches allow gross sins to go unchallenged, the Spirit is grieved and quenched (1 Jn 1:5-10). When you plead with God to have mercy on your church, be sure that God will begin with *you*. When He has searched and cleansed the sins from *your* heart, then He will release His power through you to revive others in the church. Let's get serious about sin and quit rationalizing it!

Don't be afraid to go to the Father and ask him to search you. When He does, confess and repent, "Lord, my old nature has been king of the hill. I am sorry for that. There has been pride in my heart. There has been a false spirituality. Lord, there are so many things in my life that make me a hypocrite." And Jesus will say lovingly, "You are my child; you see that you have sinned, and I'm glad you know it. Now we can get somewhere."

Chapter 2

Listening to the Voice of God

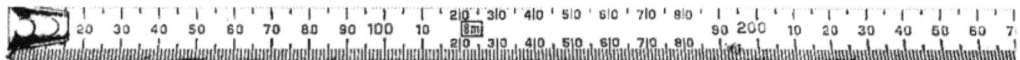

"I ask and ask," said the deacon as he chatted with his pastor one evening after the fellowship dinner. "I just cannot tell when God is answering," he added. It helps to talk with others as you seek to discern what God is saying, because we all struggle with this common problem from time to time. We pray, asking God to reveal something to us, but then we have trouble understanding how He speaks. The same is true when we are trying to discern His plan for our church. We pray earnestly, but we don't know how to hear His answers. Admittedly, it is not always easy to discern what God is saying, but He has given us some clear guidelines to follow as we learn to be better listeners.

Take a few moments to answer the following questions. (If you're unable to complete the survey, don't be discouraged - the purpose of this chapter is to help you become more proficient at recognizing God's voice.)

1. List 3 times in your life that you clearly remember God speaking to you. What did He say?

   (1)

   (2)

   (3)

2. Describe the *most recent time* that God spoke to you.
    How did you know it was God?

3. What or whom did He use to speak to you? (Check all that apply.)

    __While reading the Bible, or hearing it preached or taught
    __During prayer
    __Through the pastor or some other person
    __Through an event or circumstance
    __In my own spirit or mind
    __Other: _____
            (What?)

4. Can you identify any pattern in the way God speaks to you?

    __Mostly through the Bible and prayer
    __Through others
    __Through circumstances
    __Through my mind or in my own spirit
    __By troubling me first or making me dissatisfied

5. What is your *usual* response when you know God has spoken to you?

    __Immediately obey
    __Want to have time to test my impressions
    __Need to get confirmation from others
    __Often doubt whether I have heard correctly

How God Spoke to Individuals in the Bible

One way we grow in our understanding of how God speaks to humans is to study the *ways* He spoke to people in Bible times. Listed below are a few examples. Do you remember the events or the people involved? Can you think of other times He spoke, that are not included here?

- He spoke directly to the person.
- He spoke through dreams.
- He sent angels to deliver His message.
- He sent prophets to deliver His message.
- He spoke through the preaching and teaching of Scripture.
- He spoke as people prayed and worshiped.
- He spoke through the Holy Spirit.
- He used circumstances to speak.
- He used others to speak.

Does God still speak in these ways today? Which ones have you experienced?

Note: God is not the only one who speaks to humans. The devil also speaks, trying to lead us astray from God's will and purpose. There are several common ways he speaks, one of which is to disguise himself as an angel of light or as the Holy Spirit. He whispers into our minds, hearts, and circumstances, and even through the lips of other people. He is a master at twisting the Bible. (Do you remember how he twisted it during the temptation of Jesus in the wilderness? See Mt 4:1-11.) This is why it is ALWAYS wise to confirm your impressions through another believer – to determine whether or not it is truly God who is speaking.

We should not always accept it as truth when someone says that God has spoken to him/her. At such times, you should say to God, "Lord, confirm what they are saying in my heart and through Your Word." Don't be led astray by well-meaning people who may be convinced that their own thoughts are actually God's voice.

Lessons from Bible Characters

In the Scriptures, God spoke to certain individuals. By looking at their experiences, we can gather helpful information for ourselves.

*First, here are some general guidelines about **how** and **why** God spoke to humans:*

1. He demanded accountability when they had been disobedient.
Example: Adam and Eve. God asked them, "Where are you? Have you done what I told you not to do?"

2. He gave an explanation of the real choices that lay before them.
Example: Cain, who was upset about his offering. God told him, "if you do what is right; it will turn out to be good. If you do what is wrong, sin is at your door to catch you." (God says that we all have choices to make, and all of them are accompanied by corresponding benefits or consequences.)

3. He taught them the need for reverence in His holy presence.
Example: Moses. God spoke from a burning bush, telling Moses to remove his sandals because the place where he was standing was holy ground. (Many of us have lost our sense of the holiness of God because we do not want to face our own sins.)

4. He issued the call to follow Him.
Example: Abraham, who was called to go to a place unknown to him. (Sometimes, God doesn't speak because He knows we are not willing to obey.)

5. He gave a tough message to be delivered to someone else.
Example: Samuel, who was given a hard message to deliver to Eli about his disobedience and its consequences. (Most of us do not like to be messengers of rebuke or warning, but when God speaks, we must obey - even if it means confronting the entire church!)

6. He issued a call to mission.
Example: Isaiah saw the holiness of God. He responded with repentance. When he heard God say, "Whom shall we send, and who will go for us?" Isaiah answered bravely, "Here am I Lord, send me." (How faithful are you and your congregation in responding to God's call to mission?)

7. He gave the command to keep Jesus central in their lives.
Example: On the Mount of Transfiguration, Peter wanted to build three tabernacles; one each for Elijah, Moses, and Jesus. God's voice boomed from heaven as He enlightened the disciples, instructing them clearly that they were to listen to His Son, and to make Him central in everything. (Perhaps we have failed to hear this same message for our churches. Do we elevate Jesus in everything we do?)

8. He said religious zeal without commitment to Jesus wasn't the answer.
Example: Saul of Tarsus had great religious zeal for truth, which drove him to persecute Christians, but he was wrong. He was actually working against God's purposes, and God had to set him straight. (Sometimes our own blindness to truth makes it necessary for God to use drastic measures to get our attention!)

NOW THAT WE'VE LOOKED AT HOW AND WHY GOD SPOKE, HERE ARE SOME ADDITIONAL TRUTHS:

1. Sin and disobedience block fellowship with God. God will keep convicting us until we repent. We may have forgotten this truth. Often, God isn't speaking because unconfessed sin has led us out of fellowship with Him.

2. We can expect no other word from God until we respond to His reproof with confession and obedience. Too often, disobedience characterizes our lifestyle. Until we confront our disobedience with change, God's silence is all that we will hear. And our churches will make no progress.

3. God may have to humble us through life's difficulties to rid us of self-sufficiency and make us willing to hear. It is possible that we have not suffered enough. We may have to experience persecution and intense suffering in our country before we and our churches wake up to our spiritual need. When things are going well, we live as if we don't need God, believing ourselves to be fully capable of handling life without Him.

4. God may either speak or remain silent in order to show us that religious activity and zeal are worthless without commitment to His Lordship. We are powerless to change anyone else but ourselves. If we want our churches to change, we have to deal with the issues in our own lives first. Then our churches will be one step closer to God's plan.

5. God will remind us that nothing should compete with Jesus. He is to be our focus. Nothing should ever usurp our focus on Jesus! In life, it's easy to talk *about* Jesus without ever talking *to* Jesus. Likewise, in worship: it's easy to sing *about* Jesus without ever singing *to* Him.

6. Sometimes God will speak to us and ask us to confront a disobedient child of His. Most of us avoid the unpleasant task of confrontation. But if God asks us to do it, we must obey.

7. God may ask us to go somewhere or to do something that's outside of our comfort zone. We *prefer* our comfort zones - because they're *comfortable!* Our *comfort zones* are those places and situations that are familiar, and about which we feel competent to handle. Churches have comfort zones, too. Isn't it more comfortable to invite others to church than it is to take the gospel to them where they live and work? Of course it is. But we're supposed to be gathering on Sunday to be empowered by the Spirit so that we can go out and impact the world with the Gospel.

Do I Really Want God to Speak to Me?

"I'm not going to chapel today," said a seminary student, "because they're having an emphasis on missions, and I don't want to hear a call to missions."

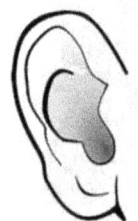

True story! Now, you might not be quite so blunt about it, but isn't there at least one area about which *you* might be reluctant to hear God speak? What might He ask *you* to do that you would be unwilling to do? It isn't far-fetched to ask, "Do I really want to hear God speak to me?" Some of us may chuckle when reading the last example, and may say, "Of *course* I want God to speak to me - as long as He says what I want to hear!"

Does fear well up in you when you think of the God of the Universe speaking to you? If so, you may need to hear this word from the Apostle John: *There is no **fear** in love. But perfect love drives out **fear**, because **fear** has to do with punishment. The one who **fears** is not made perfect in love* (1Jn. 4:18). The same verse from the New Living Translation is helpful: *Such love has no fear, because perfect love expels all fear. If we are afraid, it is for fear of punishment, and this shows that we have not fully experienced his perfect love.*

If you're afraid of what God might say or ask of you, you may not be completely convinced of His love. This is the time to ask God to examine your heart and correct any misunderstanding.

Tips for Hearing God

Although there is no easy formula for knowing how to hear God, here are some tips that we hope will help you. (Take time to read the Bible passages.)

1. Be certain you are His child (Jn 8:47; 10:3, 14).
You may not know who they are, but there are people in your church who are not born-again believers. What we can know is this: if the power of God becomes evident in our churches, those who do not know him will be convicted of their need to repent and believe in Jesus. There will be a day when some will stand before Him and hear the dreadful words, "I do not know you." On that day, it won't matter that they were active in the church. He will say, "I don't know you. I never had a personal relationship with you." This is difficult even to contemplate.

2. Your life must be one of obedience (Lk 6:46; Jas 1:22).
God will not bless disobedience. It really is just that simple. He will not bless unwillingness to do His will. He will not answer us simply because we want an answer. And He neither teaches nor leads those who are unteachable. The condition of the heart and the waywardness of lifestyle are the most common reasons why we don't hear the Lord speak.

3. You must be cleansed from all known sin and disobedience (Is 59:1-2).
Would you recognize a tick on your dog's face? It might hide for a short while, but sooner or later you'll notice it and want to remove it. It doesn't belong there, and it can be uncomfortable and even harmful to both you and your dog. This is a good reminder of the importance of dealing with every sin, even those we consider to be insignificant. God wants to remove everything in our lives that will hurt us or anyone else.

4. Spend time daily in worship, Bible study, and prayer (Acts 1:14, 24; 2:42).
It is easier to understand what someone is saying when you know their heart. Even if

they speak English in a broken Spanish accent, you can tell what they mean - if you know their heart. One reason that we need to spend time in Bible study and prayer is to get to know the heart of God. He loves to speak to us when we meet Him in prayer, worship, and Bible study. We would undoubtedly hear Him speak more often if we would spend more time listening!

5. You must be responsive to the Spirit's leadership (Jn 14:26; Acts 8:29).
Parents will readily understand this example: nothing is quite as aggravating as having to repeat instructions multiple times before a child finally obeys. In fact, some children are so used to hearing parents yell that they don't respond at all when a parent speaks normally. God doesn't like to yell, however, so we need to learn to be quiet, attentive, and obedient.

6. You must be able to discern God's leadership when He speaks through circumstances (Acts 16:6-10).
The more familiar we are with how God led His people in the Bible, the more sensitive we will be to His leading in our lives. We learn from others' experiences as well as our own. Have you noticed how the Lord repeats a lesson as many times as it takes for us to learn it? We can help one another learn by sharing what we see God doing, and how He has led us.

7. Develop the habit of humbly asking Him to speak to you (1 Sam 3:10).
We have learned that success and independence often go hand in hand. Add to that the human tendency to want to be in control of everything, and you can see why it is so easy to forget to ask God for His direction in our lives.

8. Being a good listener to the voice of God is a rational choice (Ps 85:8).
We choose whether we want to listen to God or not. Remember, however, that God does not waste time speaking when He knows we will not be obedient. Instead, He'll spend His time working on our commitment and obedience levels.

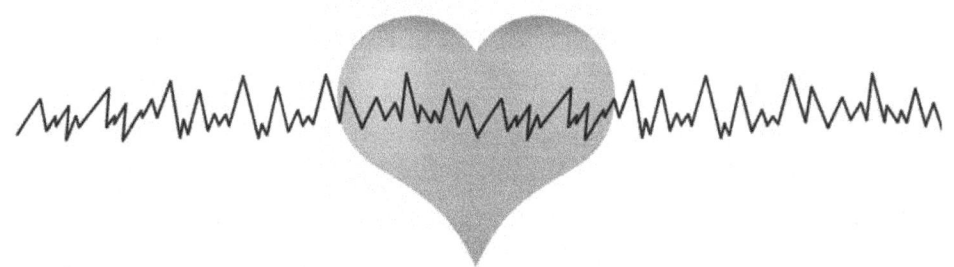

Primary Ways God Speaks to People Today

Although God is not limited in the ways He speaks to His children, there are three primary ways that He speaks, and they work in conjunction with each other. A camera mounted on a tripod is a good example. If one leg is short or absent, the camera will not be straight and the pictures will be skewed. In a similar way, when God speaks to us, all three of the following things must be in balance if we are to be assured that God is indeed speaking. The three are equally important; never emphasize one to the exclusion of another.

The three legs are as follows:

1. God speaks through His written Word, the Bible.
We also have a relationship with the Living Word, Jesus, and the Holy Spirit dwells in our hearts to help us understand God's message. To be proficient at hearing God's voice, we must be diligent students of God's Word.

2. God speaks through circumstances, events, abilities, common sense, etc.
God expects us to use our brains - for listening to other people, for reading good books, and for examining our skills and gifts. We also learn to watch for open and closed doors of opportunity as another way He guides us.

3. God speaks through inner impressions (such as how we feel in our hearts, or whether we have peace about something).
Caution: Impressions are not the same as feelings. Emotions are fickle; by themselves, they aren't trustworthy. A good way to treat feelings is to allow a few days to go by before acting on them. When you are praying about a situation, ask God to either strengthen or weaken your impressions. Be careful not to mistake your passion for the voice of God. We may be earnest, but wrong.

REMEMBER: All three of these things must be in agreement before we can be sure God is speaking to us. For example, God will never speak through our hearts or circumstances a message that is contrary to His Word. Pray; talk with others; ask God for discernment; and be encouraged to know that God truly wants to speak to you. He doesn't play hide-and-seek. If we're having difficulty hearing Him, we are usually the problem.

The Importance of Hearing God's Voice

The majority of Christians would admit to never having heard or sensed the leading of the voice of God. When something positive happens, people may believe it to be either a stroke of good luck or preordained by God. People also often believe that bad experiences are either bad luck, or evidence that God is punishing them for some sin or disobedience. Because so many seem to have difficulty hearing God speak, they cannot accept that it can *and should* be part of their everyday life. Or they believe that they personally are incapable of such an experience.

What would you do in order to be able to hear the voice of God? While God's voice may come audibly, more often it will be a moving in your heart that is unmistakably God. How do we get to the point that we hear God speak regularly? If we believe this is possible, wouldn't we go to any length to help that happen?

My (Keith) wife, Mary Ruth, is a musician. She is an accomplished pianist who also leads choirs, and whose deep love for music stirs both heart and soul as she interprets songs in American Sign Language. Music has always been a major part of her life. One of her favorite singers is Larry Gatlin, particularly his song, "All the Gold in California." I have two friends whose son plays in a band with him in Branson, Missouri. When I told them how much Mary Ruth admires Gatlin, they told me to tell her to keep her cell phone close by and turned on every day, without telling her why. They would ask their son to have Larry Gatlin call her; they knew it would thrill her. We didn't know when, however. It might be during the day, when they were on the road, or at night after a concert. It would be a challenge to convince her to keep her phone on all the time without telling her why.

I told her about the conversation with our friends, but not about the possibility of a phone call from Larry Gatlin. A few days later, I reminded her to keep her phone on at all times, because she might get a call from someone important. Several weeks went by, but she kept her phone on, even though she didn't really understand why. Even after a couple of months went by, she kept her phone on, day and night. Then, one afternoon, while she was at her arts and crafts store, her phone rang. From her reaction, the rest of us who were there knew that this was no ordinary phone call. She said, "Hello," and our friends told her someone wanted to talk to her. It was Larry Gatlin! You can imagine her expression; she even began to tremble.

When the phone call ended, the shrieks went something like, "That was Larry Gatlin! I can't believe Larry Gatlin called me! I can't believe it! And we talked for *fifteen* minutes!" Once she calmed down, she shared that they had spent that fifteen minutes talking about their common interest in music, their love of playing the piano in church, and their lives as believers. It may not sound like a typical conversation between a star and a lifelong fan, but I can tell you that experience made her day, her week, and her month. She counts it as one of the top ten highlights of her life.

I share that story as a way to remind you that Jesus, your Savior and Friend, has a gift for *you*. He is alive and He wants to speak to you. He said, "My sheep hear my voice" (Jn 10:27). In order for that to happen, however, we must do as my wife did: we must know that someone special wants to speak to us, we must keep our ear ready for the call, and we must be open to whenever and however He calls.

Gregory Frizzell writes that meditation is a form of prayer, because it is communication with God through prayerful listening. He explains that in meditation we are quietly listening for God's voice through His Word and the impressions He speaks to our hearts.[4]

Do we do all of the talking when we pray? When we say, "*Amen*," are we off and running, much like we do following the benediction at church? Meditation is a listening process that gives God a chance to speak to us. Frizzell gives practical guidelines for daily meditation to help any believer who wants a genuine relationship with Christ.

God wants us to speak to him in prayer, of course, but He also wants us to listen. He knows our every need, and desires for us to be in the center of His will. He will speak truth to us, if we will allow Him to do so. We know that He wants to speak to us; we don't know how or when He will speak. He will speak through his Word and during our worship, but He could also speak to us in the middle of the night, or while we are driving the car. If we lose our focus on Him during our daily routine, we could miss hearing Him. What a tragedy that would be!

We, the deacons and leaders of our churches, must be intentional about listening for the voice of God. We must grow in our desire to hear from Him and work to make ourselves constantly available to hear what our Shepherd wants to say to us. Once He speaks to you, you'll never be the same. Once He is allowed to lead your church, your church will never be the same. Keep your hearts open to the voice of God. It is absolutely imperative!

When you begin to seek to hear God speak, you might be surprised at how often He does just that. Because we were created to have fellowship with God, it makes perfect sense that talking and listening to Him should be our top priorities. How often and in what ways are you hearing from God?

---

[4] Gregory R. Frizzell, How to Develop a Powerful Prayer Life: The Biblical Path to Holiness and Relationship With God (Master Design: Memphis, 1999)

Hindrances to Hearing God's Voice: Satan's Schemes

Whatever God desires for His people is the opposite of what our enemy Satan wants. God wants to speak to His children, and He wants to have a loving relationship with them. Satan seeks to disrupt that relationship and to alienate people from God. As we become more aware of the enemy's tricks, we can do what it takes to maintain a close relationship with God, talking with Him as well as hearing from Him. This is why we were created, and why Jesus was sent to redeem us from sin. But, if we remain ignorant of God's goals and Satan's tactics to disrupt that relationship, we will continue to have difficulty hearing from God.

Tactics of our Arch Enemy, Satan

1. He slanders God's children when they stray from God.
Satan not only accuses God's children, filling them with guilt when they fail, he also causes other believers to use their mouths to slander and gossip. Someone rightly said that Christians tend to "shoot their wounded" rather than forgive and restore them.

Until we realize that even believers can be mouthpieces that Satan uses for slander, we are in trouble. We need to remind our people about this flaming arrow that the devil uses to attack the spirituality of a local congregation. We must stop the powers of darkness and call to account the children of God whose lips are being used by the evil one to hurt others.

2. He throws flaming arrows at us – arrows that burn, poison, and kill.
In one of the churches in our association, someone repeatedly set little fires that destroyed portions of classrooms and the fellowship hall. Though the fires were small, the damage was quite real. The church leaders didn't know if the vandal was a stranger, or someone who was affiliated with the church. One thing they did know, however, was that they had to take action to put a stop to the fires, hold the culprit accountable, and set up safeguards to make sure it never happened again.

Satan loves to start spiritual fires in the church just to keep people distracted from doing what God wants them to do. Have you ever heard a pastor say that 'putting out fires' took up a great deal of his time and energy? How very sad that the church is unaware of how Satan uses individuals to start little fires of anger and disagreement that can inflame an entire church!

We also need to be sure that we are not the ones shooting flaming arrows at our staff or other members. Church staff often wonder why members save up their criticisms or other cutting remarks until just before the worship service! A dart in the heart, a little comment or accusation, or a little "so-and-so said…" – flaming arrows!

3. He uses the love of money as a root to introduce all kinds of evil.
Satan uses the love of money to undermine the financial base of local congregations. How often do churches focus on low offerings instead of God's power and calling to reach the masses? Does everyone in your congregation tithe? Does the church tithe its own income? Churches can be self-centered spenders. Ask yourself, "How much of our budget is for outreach, and how much is for us?" Examine these things closely, because the love of money can derail a church and its ministry. Satan plants the subtle love of money in all kinds of ways.

4. He sows his followers among the good wheat.
Believe it or not, some church leaders have been placed there by Satan himself to harm and disrupt the people of God. It is urgent that we remember what Jesus said: *"not everyone who cries 'Lord, Lord,' will enter the kingdom of heaven, but only he who does the will of my Father in heaven. Many will say to me 'Lord, Lord, have I not prophesied in your name, and cast out many demons,' and I will tell them plainly, 'I never knew you, away from me you evil doers'"* (Mt 7:21).

In some churches, Satan has planted the preacher. The result is a congregation that is bleeding and torn to shreds, as if a wild animal had attacked an unsuspecting flock of lambs. In other churches, wonderful men and women of God serve faithfully, but certain members tear the church apart. The evil one is powerful and subtle.

5. He tempts us, and he is very persistent.
Did you know that temptations are unique to the individual being tempted? What tempts you may not tempt someone else. Satan uses our weaknesses to engineer our temptations. He knows how to quote scripture, a tactic he used against Jesus in the wilderness temptation. Anyone who does not have a correct understanding of Biblical truth is susceptible to such deception. All of us need to know when someone is teaching or preaching something other than the Word of God.

6. He steals the word of God out of our minds and hearts.
Our enemy snatches the Word of God from the minds and hearts of non-believers easily, but he also knows how to steal from believers. Most of us are not good listeners, and we are all prone to distractions even when the Bible is faithfully preached to us!

7. He uses unresolved anger to gain a foothold in our lives.
Unresolved anger between believers is an open invitation to Satan to establish a foothold in our lives (Eph 4:26-27). In many of our churches, there are people who will not talk to one another because of some bitterness or resentment that resulted when someone got mad.

8. He traps people in the midst of quarrels, capturing them to do his will.
Conflict among the family of believers is probably the number one way Satan destroys churches today! He traps us in the midst of our quarrels, capturing the church by distracting it from the worship and mission of God.

9. He prowls around like a roaring lion, looking for someone to devour.
Satan is ever on the lookout for some person or church to devour. If you knew there was a hungry lion stalking your children, wouldn't you take immediate action? Of course you would. So, why is it that we are not constantly armed and ready to defend our churches from this mortal enemy?

10. He works to lead us and the world astray, away from God.
Satan doesn't really care how busy Christians are, as long as they are not winning people to faith in Christ. Nor does he care how religious we are, as long as we aren't taking time to worship and serve God. When "busy-ness" takes the place of yieldedness to the Lord, religiosity can replace true commitment. Soon self-centeredness replaces God-centeredness, and stagnation replaces spirituality.

11. He is our accuser before God.
He accuses us before God, hurling condemnation at us. Many believers are crippled in their life of faith because of guilt over failure and their lack of knowledge about the grace and forgiveness of God. The devil also enlists us to be accusers of others! How often do we gripe and complain about others, instead of bowing in prayer and interceding for them?

12. He masquerades as an angel of light.
Satan and his servants masquerade as servants of righteousness. He loves to play Holy Spirit, whispering suggestions as well as condemnation into the ears of believers, trying to lead them away from the will of God. His servants like to play the Holy Spirit in the lives of others, too, using tactics like control and religious superiority to intimidate others and elevate themselves.

13. He torments believers.
Satan has many tools in his arsenal with which to torment God's children. He can bring sickness upon us, and then accuse us of being sinful. He causes us to doubt the love and faithfulness of God when we are in the midst of trials. He torments us over past failures and present difficulties. He keeps our minds busy with worries, plans, and regrets. Mental and emotional torments of all kinds haunt us when Satan is attacking. If you have ever seen a movie clip of someone down on the ground, surrounded by attackers who mercilessly kick and hit him, then you have seen a good picture of how the devil loves to hurt believers! We need each other's help along the pathway of life.

14. He is a liar and the father of lies.
It's a sad thing when Christians are entrapped by the father of lies, becoming channels through which he can perpetuate his lies. Sometimes those lies take the form of gossip; sometimes it is hypocrisy, which may be his best tool for keeping unbelievers disillusioned with the church.

15. He is the prince of this world.
The world marches in step with him; unfortunately, so do some believers!

16. He is a schemer.
He is diabolically clever, and smarter than any of us will ever be. He uses us in his destructive plans, and we are all vulnerable to his poison. No human can outwit him or figure out where he will attack next. The only safe position is close to the side of Jesus. Have you ever noticed in Jesus' prayer for His disciples and for us (John 17) that He prayed repeatedly for our protection from the evil one? We should pray this prayer daily, for ourselves and for others.

17. He rules over the powers of darkness in the world, and over the spiritual forces of evil in the heavenly realms, too.
Satan loves secrecy. It's no coincidence that one of the church's major weaknesses is a tendency among its leaders to sweep things under the rug. They prefer to try to forget or hide the issues, instead of bringing them out into the light to expose them. We are so

concerned about hurting someone's feelings that we will let our church suffer just to keep some people happy! The power of darkness loves that.

Leaders and individuals must understand what problems arise when we listen to Satan and fall for his schemes rather than listening to and following God. Are you aware of Satan's tactics in your church? Do you know what to do about his attacks? The weapons for his defeat are spiritual ones. They are not the weapons of this world. Study Eph. 6:10-18 carefully so you will know what the armor of God is and how to put it on daily.[5] This will help you walk with your eyes wide open in the world, and your ears tuned in to the voice of God.

---

[5] See <u>Time for a Checkup: Assessing Our</u> Progress in Spiritual Growth, by Dr. Alice Cullinan. (CLC Publication, Ft. Washington, PA, 1993), p. 63.

Chapter 3

Understanding Personality Types and Spiritual Gifts

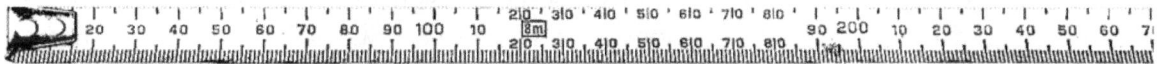

"Why can't he ever make up his mind?"

"Does she have to be right about *everything*?"

"Why can't they see this from my perspective?"

"He seems to say everything he *thinks* about!"

Do these thoughts ever pop up in your mind when you are working with others? Have you wondered how people could be so wrong, yet think they're right? Have you noticed how some people like to talk an idea to death while others want to hurry up and make a decision? If you have served in any capacity in the church, then you realize just how different people are! What we call "worship wars" - disagreements about music styles - is mostly a matter of different preferences. Our personality differences affect the way we pray, worship God, and study the Bible. They also affect our comfort levels when people expect us to serve in a variety of ways, simply because we are deacons. One person will be overjoyed to read the Scriptures or pray during worship, while another will be filled with dread. What is causing the differences? The answer is simple yet profound: differences in our personalities affect our preferences, our interactions, our leadership styles and our comfort levels. When you consider everyone's unique life experiences and their differing talents and spiritual gifts, it's a wonder we get along at all!

Sociologists, psychologists, and theologians have all struggled to understand these differences. We are approaching a broad subject, one that is beyond the scope of this book. But, we will provide basic facts and principles to help you understand yourself and others in the church where you serve.

Personality Types and Their Impact on the Church

When I (Alice) was a student in seminary working on a PhD in Psychology, I took a class in personality theories. The first thing that grabbed my attention was how many different theories there are! There is definitely a great deal of interest in what makes people tick. We wonder why we think and act and react as we do. We wonder what roles heredity and environment play in making us different. Is our behavior learned from others, or are we captive to our genetic makeup? How is it that identical twins can sometimes be so different in how they view and react to the world? What is that thing called *chemistry* that happens between people, either drawing them close or inexplicably putting them at odds? While social scientists spend their lives trying to answer these questions, we will restrict ourselves to some basic things a deacon needs to understand, beginning with "personality types." Every church is made up of people who have different personality types, and there are many different personality types in the Bible.

See if you can identify the following Biblical characters: *

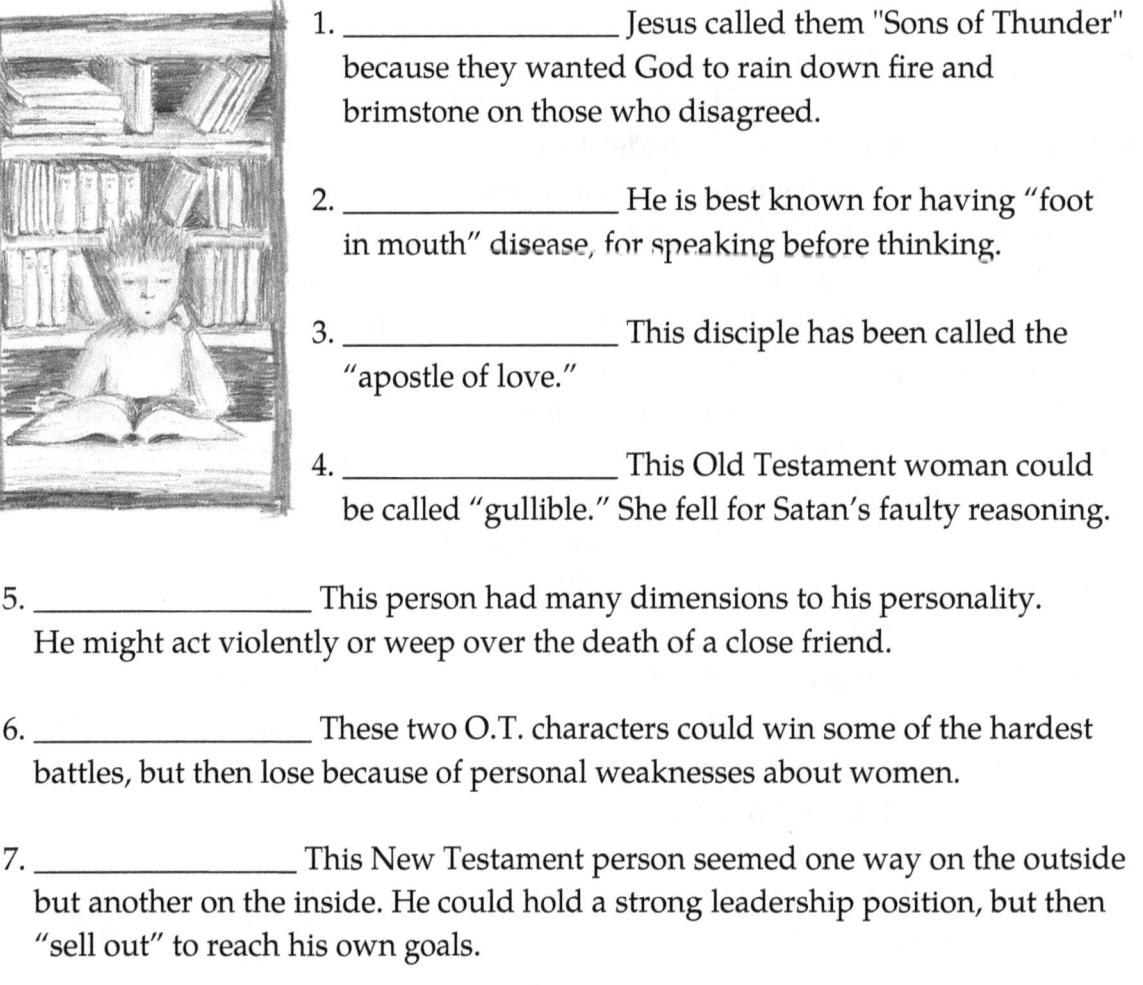

1. _____ Jesus called them "Sons of Thunder" because they wanted God to rain down fire and brimstone on those who disagreed.

2. _____ He is best known for having "foot in mouth" disease, for speaking before thinking.

3. _____ This disciple has been called the "apostle of love."

4. _____ This Old Testament woman could be called "gullible." She fell for Satan's faulty reasoning.

5. _____ This person had many dimensions to his personality. He might act violently or weep over the death of a close friend.

6. _____ These two O.T. characters could win some of the hardest battles, but then lose because of personal weaknesses about women.

7. _____ This New Testament person seemed one way on the outside but another on the inside. He could hold a strong leadership position, but then "sell out" to reach his own goals.

8. _____ This O.T. woman was so self-giving that she was willing to put her mother-in-law's needs above her own.

9. _____ This O.T. man is best known for being the kind of friend everyone needs.

10. _____ This N.T. person could stand up to a strong fellow leader and tell him when he was not obeying the will of the Lord.

See the end of the chapter for the answers.

The Bible is filled with people of every imaginable personality type. From their stories, we can learn a great deal by considering their differences, yet noticing how God could still use each one of them to accomplish His purpose. Our challenge is to learn how to work with one another even when preferences or personality conflicts disrupt the harmony. Paul and Barnabus had a serious conflict over John Mark. John Mark had quit before completing the first missionary journey, but wanted to accompany the apostles on the second one. Paul and Barnabas actually parted company for a while, because they could not agree. But they did not let their conflict keep them from their missionary goals, nor did they allow it to become a permanent rift between them. In some of his later writings, Paul mentions how valuable John Mark was to his ministry.

Personality Types: The Myers-Briggs Type Indicator

The Meyers-Briggs Type Indicator is a tool for assessing personality types. If conflict is interfering with the ministry of your church, it will be beneficial to do a study focused on the differences between personality types. Books, guides, and online resources are plentiful. In the meantime, here is a short overview of their concepts.

According to Myers-Briggs,[6] each of us relates to the world and to one another out of our personalities and preferences, some of which we were taught and some we inherited. Myers and Briggs described these differences according to four categories:

- Introvert(I)/Extravert(E)
- Sensing(S)/iNtuitive(N)
- Thinking(T)/Feeling(F)
- Judging(J)/Perceiving(P)

What follows are brief synopses of each type.

Introvert(I)/Extravert(E)

The descriptors actually have little to do with our social approach to others. It has more to do with how we prefer to interact with the world and how we receive energy. The extravert (**E**) engages others easily; the introvert (**I**) will not open up as quickly. **E's** are energized by being with people - the more the better. Being around too many people for too long will drain the **I**, who gains energy by being alone and quiet. Imagine a deacons' meeting: the **E's** talk as they think, which doesn't give the **I's** time to reflect before they speak. Having to remain quiet for too long drains the **E**, while the **I's** are beside themselves when there is constant talking and no quiet. Everybody gets frustrated.

Just this one category of differences in personality is the source of a lot of misunderstanding and conflict in our churches, but there are three more! On top of that, there are all of the various combinations that can occur because each personality is some mixture of the four categories. Now you can see that people really do have very different perspectives, and that they really aren't "just trying to be difficult," which is how we sometimes describe those whose opinions differ from our own.

---

[6] Isabel Briggs Myers and Peter Myers, <u>Gifts Differing: Understanding Personality Type</u> (Davies-Black Publishing: Mountain View Calif., 1980. Also see: http://www.myersbriggs.org/my-mbti-personality-type/mbti-basics/

Sensing(S)/iNtuitive(N)

In this category, there are **S's** who prefer specific answers to specific questions and like to concentrate on what they're doing at the moment, rather than what might be coming in the future. They would rather work with facts and figures than with ideas and theories, and get frustrated if they aren't given clear instructions or directions. The **S** loves to see the tangible results of his or her work. In contrast, the **N** can think of several things at once and is sometimes accused of being absent-minded. They love to dream about what the future might hold and hate boring details. They are always asking, "What does that mean?" and tend to give general answers to most questions.

Thinking(T)/Feeling(F)

This Myers-Briggs category has to do with how we prefer to make decisions. **T's** remain calm and objective in situations where everyone else is upset. They decide based on what is fair and true, rather than what makes people happy. At times, they are more firm-minded than gentle-hearted. They don't mind making difficult decisions even though they are sometimes accused of being uncaring; and they don't mind telling others when they disagree with them. **F's**, on the other hand, want to take others' feelings into account when making a decision. They are concerned with meeting others' needs, which can leave them vulnerable to those who would take advantage of them. They prefer harmony and will do everything in their power to avoid conflict. They are quick to make amends if they have hurt someone. They are often accused of taking things too personally. Can you see how these differences account for many of the conflicts that come up in deacons' meetings ... or in the church as a whole?

Judging(J)/Perceiving(P)

This category can be a source of major conflict. **J's** are organized, on time, like to follow a schedule and hate surprises. They like to make lists and follow them, appreciate a well-thought out agenda, and can have strong opinions. They want to see results, and will work hard to complete tasks ... on time! **P's**, on the other hand, hate to plan, preferring to keep their options open. They are spontaneous; they like to turn work into play. They can be very disorganized, which often results in the necessity of last minute spurts of energy to meet deadlines.

As you think about the different personality types, keep in mind just how many opportunities for conflict are provided by the variety of trait combinations. Myers-Briggs worked out a detailed analysis of how these traits combine. If you are interested to know more, you should explore their work. Let it suffice to say that personality differences are at the root of many conflicts and misunderstandings that plague our churches. But when we understand the strengths and weaknesses of each personality type and combinations of types, we can plan accordingly and make the most of our differences. Instead of suffering, our churches can benefit from these differences!

Taking A Closer Look at Myself

Most of us are not as self-aware as we should be, at least when it comes to understanding our own strengths and weaknesses. It is amazing how someone who is  capable and smart can view him/herself in an entirely different light. One of the most heart-breaking things about people who suffer from bulimia (a self-enforced regurgitation of food as a method of avoiding weight gain) is that when they look into a mirror, they see themselves as fat, even though they are thin. Intelligent people may feel stupid and inadequate, and obnoxious people may believe everybody loves them! What's going on? One's self-viewing lens can be much in need of cataract surgery! Many different things affect self-concept. When we are young, we see ourselves through the words and reactions of our parents toward us. As we grow older, others become the mirrors through which we see ourselves. We begin to develop 'tapes' - recordings of others' words - which we play back repeatedly to ourselves until those words become our reality. WHO we are is who we THINK we are, whether the facts are based in reality or not.

As part of my (Keith) ministry as an Associational Missionary, I was trained as a Career Consultant for the Baptist State Convention of North Carolina. What a great opportunity! My consultations were primarily with ministers who had been terminated or who were at a point in their lives when they wanted to re-evaluate their call and future course in life. I have been able to use these same materials with deacons and other leaders of the church to help them learn more about themselves, so they can work more effectively in ministry.

Each of us ought to be as self-aware as possible. Haven't most of us asked ourselves,

"Why do I always do that?" Sometimes we don't ask, though, because our behaviors and reactions have become so much a part of our lives.

How do you function in your duties as a deacon? Are you dominant? Do you have to be in charge? Do you always have to have your way, or do you sit back and let others make decisions? Have there ever been issues that caused you to disengage entirely? Are you discerning, able to see the underlying problems that may be beneath the surface of a conflict? Understanding why you react in certain ways can often be explained by obtaining a fairly objective picture of the traits that make up your personality. It is also helpful to understand the experiences and relationships that have formed and shaped you through the years. Such insights will help you relate to others more effectively in your leadership role. I am convinced that the more we know about ourselves, the more effective we will be as leaders. Tools for exploring personality types and traits are readily available.

These exercises may give you insight. In the next few weeks, try to make time to complete them.

1. *Make a list of your strengths and weaknesses.* Which ones seem to come naturally (as if they are inherited), and which ones have you learned?

2. *Ask friends or family who know you well to list your strengths and weaknesses.* Ask them to be as forthright as possible, and to be available for questions if you have them. It is best if you read their list when they are not present. You can ask for clarification later if necessary.

3. *Write an autobiography of your life.* Although this may take significant time and effort, it is an invaluable tool that will reveal patterns and traits to help you in your journey to self-understanding. One option is to include only the major events, both good and bad, that have impacted your life (and how).

4. *Make a list of your pet peeves:* things people say or do that easily cause you to react. Also list some personality traits in others that conflict with yours. Take time to examine what causes these negative reactions in you and why they do so. You may want to ask someone who knows you well to share with you what he or she considers to be traits in your personality that cause others to react negatively.

5. *List these things:* What you love. What you hate. What stresses you. What relaxes you. How you personally deal with whatever upsets you.

Study what you have written and talk it over with a trusted friend or counselor. Your answers may lead you to greater self-awareness. When we operate from a position of strength and self-awareness, we are more likely to succeed and relate well to others. Your deacon body will be more effective when everyone becomes aware of one another's strengths and when everyone leads and ministers from that vantage point.

These exercises may give you insight.

1 Make a list of your strengths and weaknesses.

2 Ask friends or family who know you well to list your strengths and weaknesses.

3 Write an autobiography of your life.

4 Make a list of your pet peeves.

5 List things you love, hate, stress over, relax with.

UNDERSTANDING SPIRITUAL GIFTS

If personality differences play an important role in our relationship with others, then it seems obvious that our spiritual gifts also play an important role in helping us  determine our ministry to others. Not all of us have the same gift(s), of course, so our ministries will not look alike. Deacons are called to serve, but each should serve out of their giftings. Unfortunately, newly elected deacons are often quickly discouraged by impossible expectations, because sometimes church staff and/or members expect each of them to possess every gifting listed in the Bible. For example, when a church implements a "deacon of the week" plan, every deacon, in turn, may be asked to read the Scripture or lead in prayer during a worship service. While the intention may be admirable, the church staff and deacon board should discuss certain questions, such as:

- † Should we expect more service from a deacon than another church member?
- † How can we be wise about our expectations?
- † Should every deacon be expected to lead in worship?
- † Do our deacons know their spiritual gifts, talents and abilities? Shouldn't they be serving in those areas where God has gifted them?

Spiritual gifts inventories and books about spiritual gifts are abundant. Every church should have materials and learning opportunities available for all members. Such learning opportunities should be presented on a regular basis, perhaps every year or two. It is important to keep in mind the importance of placing people in leadership positions according to their gifts, talents, abilities, and interests. Someone may WANT to serve in a particular place, but they may not have the gifts or abilities for the work. Someone who has been elected and ordained to the diaconate doesn't automatically become a multi-talented genius who knows all things and can do all things! The topic of spiritual gifts is another broad one that is beyond the scope this book, but in our brief treatment of the subject we do hope to inspire you to continue your study and seek additional training if necessary.

What does the Bible mean by "spiritual gifts"? Sometimes the word "gift" causes us to think that spiritual gifts are something we receive apart from the giver, like a birthday present. A closer study of the scriptures, however, suggests that the *gift* is actually a part of the *Giver* Himself. The Miriam-Webster Dictionary is helpful here: a "gift" is "a special ability; a notable capacity, talent, or *endowment*; something voluntarily transferred by one person to another without compensation." [7] The word "endowment" is most helpful when it comes to understanding spiritual gifts.

Imagine the following scenario:

> *Bill is a very talented teacher who is about to die. He gathers a group of his former students who themselves have become teachers. He shares with them that he is dying from cancer, but wants to ensure that his legacy will live on. To accomplish this, Bill is going to give each one of them a gift that will help them become even greater teachers. One by one, he calls each former student to himself to present his gift. "To you, John, I give my ability to relate to students, and to know who needs encouragement and who needs strict discipline." To another he says, "Mary, I give you my strength to deal with difficult parents who challenge and criticize you. I give you my ability to change those adversaries into friends." And to another, "Tom, I give you my ability to organize your lessons and your weekly schedule in order to accomplish more than you presently do."*

You might be thinking, "That would be great ... if it were actually possible." In the case of spiritual gifts, it *is* possible. Bill's wish, of course, is humanly impossible. But nothing is impossible for our Great Teacher, the Holy Spirit. Sent by Jesus, the Spirit comes to us, indwells us, and manifests Himself through us. Our Teacher gives Himself *to us* in order to work God's grace and perfect will *through us*! What a joy to discover which part of Himself He has bequeathed to us!

In essence, we are endowed with the Spirit Himself. Our abilities are actually *His abilities*, working in and through us. They are NOT *our* abilities at all, but the Spirit who works successful ministry through our lives. Now you see how important it is to discover your gifts and learn how to cooperate with the Spirit in your life and ministry. Instead of asking, "What are my spiritual gifts?" we should ask, "How does the Holy Spirit want to manifest (reveal) Himself through me?" If my gift is teaching, for instance, that means the Spirit has decided to manifest Himself through me when I teach. Teaching is not a gift apart from Him, because He is the one actually doing the teaching, through me, using me as His channel to bless others.

---

[7] Merriam-Webster Dictionary (http://www.merriam-webster.com)

One day, I (Alice) heard a former student of mine preach, and he used a great illustration of this principle. He had always liked playing basketball, he said, but  he wasn't very good at it. Then he said, "But, if I could somehow *morph* Michael Jordan on the inside, you would be astonished by my ability to play basketball!" Even though the word "morph" isn't in the Bible, it's a great description of the concept of the indwelling of the Holy Spirit. The Spirit lives in the heart of every believer. He wants to reveal Himself to the world through us. To accomplish that, He works to empower believers to live the life of service to which they have been called. Our part in this ministry partnership with God is to yield fully to His leadership.

BASIC PRINCIPLES ABOUT SPIRITUAL GIFTS

If you decide to broaden your understanding about spiritual gifts, you will find that there are plenty of opinions about what the gifts are and are not. No matter how much you study the topic, *the following basic principles will serve you well.*

1. Spiritual gifts aren't the same as inherited talents.
Both are useful for serving the Lord, but we should know the difference. Sometimes a spiritual gift is delivered by way of one's talent. For example, a musician who has the spiritual gift of encouragement may find that his or her music often encourages others. Likewise, an artist might be an instrument of the Spirit for teaching. Sometimes a pastor, whose spiritual gift is preaching, and who also has a talent for singing, will break into song in the middle of a sermon.

2. God *wants* us to know how He has gifted us.
He wants us to know how He wants to reveal Himself through us. If we are unaware of our gifting and God's desire to use it within the body of Christ, it is possible that we might never fulfill our true calling, because we think we are supposed to serve the church in some other capacity.

3. There are different gifts, and the Spirit chooses the vessels.
The Spirit alone makes these decisions. Our job is to discover His choice for us. We will share some prerequisites for discovering your gift(s) later in this chapter.

4. The Spirit has gifted every Christian with at least one gift.
No believer has been left out. The Spirit wants every member of the body serving other members and the world as a whole.

5. No gift is elevated above another.
God forbids envy. It is important to cooperate with the Spirit's work in you. Never waste your time - or the Lord's - envying the Spirit's work in someone else.

6. The gifts are given to benefit the Body, and accomplish God's purposes.
We know that God has a plan, but we may forget that we can thwart that plan if we refuse to yield ourselves to Him.

7. Each of us is a part of the Body of Christ; we all need one another's gifts.
If one member of the Body withholds his/her spiritual gift(s), all of the body suffers. Remember the last time you stubbed your toe? One little member *can* cause the whole body to suffer! Our bodies are made up of a variety of parts. When any part stops working, our bodies can compensate, but isn't it best if all the parts work as they were designed to do?

8. Each congregation has the gifts needed to accomplish God's will.
We may not often see this truth in action. A church may be in need of more teachers. Those who fill the gaps left by others' refusals to serve may feel inadequate or frustrated. Sometimes, churches start a ministry just because "all the other churches are doing it." Church fads come and go, and whatever is trending may tempt other congregations to add a program or new personnel just because they see another church doing so.

9. One of Satan's strategies is to keep us ignorant of our spiritual gifts.
When any of his strategies succeed, our ministries will be ineffective and we will be more likely to experience burnout. You may have heard someone say, "I would rather burn out than rust out." What they don't realize is that when you're *out* – you're *out!* Whether you're *out* because you work too much, or you're *out* because you don't work at all – you're still *out!* Let's help our members understand God's giftings and God's expectations. God cannot and will not bless a congregation filled with disobedient members who either don't know or won't use their spiritual gifts!

10. One gift may manifest in different ways.
One person with the gift of teaching may work effectively with children, while another person with the gift of teaching is better suited to work with adults. And, another

person with the gift of teaching might serve in the realm of music, while another person may serve by teaching others how to witness or pray. The Spirit is quite creative with the use of the gifts that He entrusts to His children. Reflecting on His ministry to us (Counselor, Comforter, Helper, Advocate, Intercessor, Teacher, etc.) will give you a glimpse of how He wants to use His children. Teaching, encouraging, comforting, exhorting, rebuking and strengthening are some obvious things He wants us to do!

11. We must be nurtured by the Holy Spirit, the "River of Living Water."
(See Jn 4:13-14, 7:38-39.) Without the Spirit's empowerment, the Spirit's gift in us will be burdensome and ineffective. Ministry performed in our own strength will not only fail, it will drain us spiritually. This results in believers who tire of serving. Imagine going to God in prayer one day and getting a pre-recorded message that said, "We're sorry, but we're unable to answer your prayers right now. Please leave a message." We know that will never happen! Just so, when we are filled with the Holy Spirit and letting Him live His life through us, we will never tire of serving.

12. No individual Christian has all of the gifts of the Spirit.
Most of us are gifted in one particular way for the Spirit's use, while some will experience different giftings at different times in their lives, according to the needs of the Body. We should keep in mind, however, that Paul encouraged us to desire certain gifts, especially ones that build up the Body of Christ. It never hurts to ask!

13. God requires our commitment if He is going to use us in His service.
Commitment is a requirement for successful service. Talents may or may not coincide with spiritual gifts, but we should be committed to faithfully serving God with all of them! If I have to choose, however, because of time or energy constraints, I should always put God's gifts ahead of my talents!

For a better understanding of these principles, study and pray through these passages of Scripture:
- ✞ 1 Corinthians 12
- ✞ Ephesians 4:12-14
- ✞ 1 Timothy 4:14
- ✞ Romans 11:29

14. Grieving or quenching the Spirit renders us unfruitful.
To *grieve* the Spirit means to allow anything in our lives that saddens Him: sinful activities, wrong choices, or neglecting His Word and your relationship with Him does grieve Him. It is helpful to take a spiritual inventory regularly by spending time praying and asking Him to reveal ways in which you may have grieved Him. To *quench* the Spirit means to stifle Him, to stop Him from expressing Himself through you. "Putting out the fire" is another way to describe quenching. Have you ever had the urge to say, "Amen!" or shout, "Praise the Lord!" in worship but didn't for fear of what others might think? If so, you have quenched the Spirit. It is easy for us to grieve and quench the Spirit. We must become increasingly sensitive to Him.

15. God uses our gifts and talents for building up the Body of Christ in the faith and for bringing the unsaved to faith in Christ Jesus.
Are your gifts and talents being used in your church to help others grow in their relationship with God? Are you allowing the Spirit to use your talents to reach out to a world of people who do not know Him?

16. Don't neglect your gifts, either willfully or out of ignorance.
Such neglect harms the spiritual life of individuals and congregations alike. Failure to serve out of your gifts may actually hinder someone else's spiritual growth! Be diligent in faithfulness to the Spirit and to His calling.

17. Once bestowed, a spiritual gift cannot be lost. The gift might lie dormant, however, because the gift-bearer is unwilling to yield to God.
When someone recommits his/her life to Jesus, the Spirit will re-awaken the dormant gift to once again bless the Body.

For a better understanding of these principles, study and pray through these passages of Scripture: 1 Cor 12; Eph 4:12-14; 1 Tim 4:14; Rom 11:29.

Prerequisites for Discovering Your Spiritual Gift(s)

Even when the reading is finished, the classes attended, and the spiritual inventories have been taken, some will continue to be unsuccessful in discerning how God has gifted them. When that is the case, it is time to look at *four prerequisites that must be met before the Spirit will reveal a person's gifting:*

1. You must be a born-again child of God.
You must have the Spirit of God living within. We know that it is possible for someone to be a church member, but not a believer. If you don't have the Spirit, you won't be able to discover your spiritual gift, because you don't have one yet.

2. You must be allowing Jesus to be Lord of your life.
Is your lifestyle one that is committed to Jesus: obedient and yielded to the Spirit? If you are not honoring Jesus as the Lord of your life, the Holy Spirit will not honor you.

3. You must be willing to use the spiritual gift you have been given.
Are you allowing the Spirit free reign to use you as He sees fit? If you ask for the Spirit's revelation with the attitude, "Show me first, and I'll let you know if I'm interested," then you should know that the heavens will remain silent! He knew before you asked that you were unwilling to hear the answer.

4. You must be active in a local body of believers.
The Spirit often works outside the church, but the focus of His gifts is the building up of the Body of Christ *"until we all reach unity in the faith and in the knowledge of the Son of God and become mature, attaining to the whole measure of the fullness of Christ"* (Eph 4:13).

Reasons for Failure to Find or Use One's Spiritual Gift(s)

Failure to discover one's spiritual gifting is most often due to the fact that the prerequisites haven't been met, but there are other things that can prevent it.

Here are some common blockages:

1. Disobedience or unconfessed sin.
It isn't popular to talk about sin – nonetheless, a believer who isn't walking in holiness and purity shouldn't expect the Holy Spirit to use his or her life as a vessel for His ministry. This is a key truth that is often neglected.

2. Unwillingness to allow the Spirit free reign.
Humility and willingness are foundational to effective service. Therefore, sins like stubbornness, pride, jealousy, and unforgiveness are not only *alien*, they are *harmful* to the Body of Christ. The Spirit will quietly take a back seat as long as sin is allowed to rule a person's life.

3. Lack of faith and dependence upon the Lord.
Sometimes a believer discovers his/her gift, but then tries to serve in his/her own strength or for his/her own purposes. When a believer resists what the Spirit wants to do, things do not work as they should.

4. Unbelief or doubt that all Christians are gifted by the Spirit for ministry.
Certainly, there are plenty of inactive church members who prefer being *attenders* and *sponges of blessings*. The Spirit has no Christian jobs for people in the bleachers. There are no civilians; only soldiers. Everyone is in the game; everyone should fight the fight.

5. Spiritual burnout.
Attempting to accomplish the Lord's work with mere human power invariably leads to discouragement. There are some very determined "servants" out there, but even they will reach the point where "a little time off" seems like a good idea. It is a simple equation: giving out more than taking in (spiritually) = burnout! Whenever we run on 'self-energy' instead of the Spirit's power, we will burn out.

Preparing Your Heart to Hear From the Spirit

Since the Spirit determines the giftings, it is the Spirit with whom we need to be in tune. More simply put, we need to be walking with the Spirit to be used by Him.

Here are some suggestions for success:

1. Learn how to enthrone Christ as Lord of each day and every situation.
This is accomplished by an act of the will, a definite prayer of commitment, made every morning. "Lord, this day is your day. By faith, I submit my life and my decisions to You. You are my King; I am your servant. Guide me and I will follow. Convict me and I will repent. Teach me, for I am your student." You may use this suggested prayer, but you'll probably want to design your own now that you have the basic idea. Nothing pleases the Spirit more than our willing submission to the Lordship of Christ in every aspect of our lives.

2. Make it a habit to spend time in Bible reading and prayer every day.
It is important to spend time with the Lord and in His Word before you begin the day. Reading even one chapter of the Bible and worshipping and praying for five minutes can make all the difference in how your day goes. If you have more time later in the day, by all means - read and pray and worship more!

3. Keep your sins confessed and your heart cleansed.
Nothing short-circuits the power of God more than failing to deal with sins. We can't walk in the light when there is darkness in our hearts.

4. Be actively involved in a local church.
Use your abilities and gifts to benefit others. See that your focus is not "What can my church do for me?" but rather "How can I best serve the Lord here in this place?"

5. Learn how to be obedient to the Spirit's promptings.
Learn to hear his voice. When you do, respond immediately (see Chapter Two).

Gauging Our Obedience

How can we gauge our obedience? Heb 4:12 reminds us that the Spirit uses the Scripture to help us discern our motives and actions. Scripture is the surgical instrument that will remove what needs to go. It is the light that illuminates the dark places in our hearts and minds, the balm that mends what's broken and heals all wounds. In your life, does the Spirit use the Scripture to minister to you?

Examining the Effects of Our Service

When others are being blessed, challenged, and comforted, etc., that is an indication that the Spirit is able to flow through us for ministry – hearts are only truly touched when it is the Spirit doing the ministry! When we are walking with the Spirit, we will be aware how desperately we need Him. When we are walking with the Spirit, there will be humility instead of pride, meekness and submission instead of stubborn willfulness. When we are walking with the Spirit, the fruit of the Spirit will be manifested in and through our lives (Gal 5:22-23).

Asking the Right Questions

Write down your answers to these questions.

1. If you could do anything to improve your church, and you knew it would be successful, what would you do?

2. If you could be assured of success, what position in the church would you fill or what ministry would you choose?

3. What are your hobbies? What other things do you really enjoy doing, even if you can't do them very often?

4. With what age-group(s) do you enjoy working?

5. What spiritual or personal abilities have others said that you have? Do others express appreciation for one ministry or activity that you do more than another?

6. If you could have any gift(s) you wanted, which would you choose? Why? How would you use the gift(s)?

Discovering Your Spiritual Gift(s)

There are, of course, no magic formulas. No book, workshop, or inventory can guarantee you will discover your spiritual gifts by following their suggestions. What  you *can* be sure of is that the Spirit wants to reveal His plans for your life and ministry in the kingdom. He, too, may use books, workshops, or inventories, along with many other creative methods to reveal His will and purpose. As we learn to (1) search the scriptures, (2) spend time in worship and prayer, (3) keep our sins confessed, and (4) maintain an attitude of humility and dependence, we can be assured that He will honor our search for truth about our gifts.

Once you have answered the six questions above, reflect on the following to determine whether the key to discovering your gifts might be in the answers you gave.

1. Often our own desires/aspirations for serving are clues about our gifts.
Remember that our motives must be pure. If you want to be a teacher, for instance, your motive must be the building up of the church for the glory of the Lord - NOT the building up of your own reputation.

2. What spiritual abilities have others seen in your life?
How have others been blessed or encouraged by your ministry? Do you receive thanks or compliments for some particular thing you do? There may be a theme to these messages. Don't forget to tell others how they bless you - they might be trying to discern their spiritual gifts, too.

3. Begin to volunteer and minister in some different areas.
Serve in ways that you THINK might be your area of giftedness. Confirmation will come in time, if that is where God wants you to serve. You will be blessed, as will those to whom you minister.

4. The presence or absence of a gift will be confirmed by experience.
It will result in lives being built up spiritually. When you engage in the Spirit's ministry for your life, you will experience His blessing. You will feel a sense of purpose, satisfaction, and blessing that you can't explain. In other words, as you allow Him to use you, you will be blessed!

You will be delightfully surprised at how much smoother and more enjoyable your service for the Lord will be, once you understand your own personality and spiritual gifts. Likewise, a team whose members are both self-aware and aware of each other's personality traits and spiritual gifts is a team prepared for God to use!

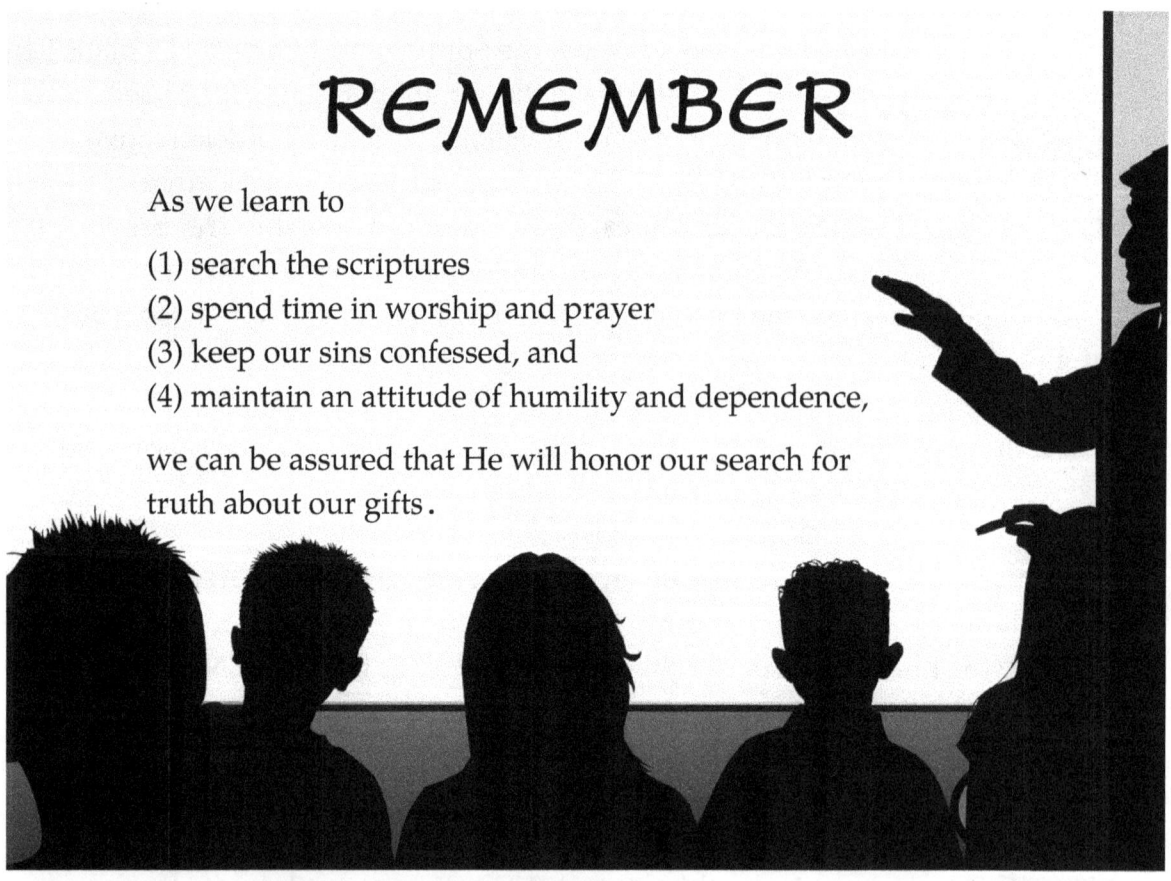

REMEMBER

As we learn to

(1) search the scriptures
(2) spend time in worship and prayer
(3) keep our sins confessed, and
(4) maintain an attitude of humility and dependence,

we can be assured that He will honor our search for truth about our gifts.

*Answers to the fill-in-the-blank questions on page 56: (1) James and John (2) Peter (3) John (4) Eve (5) David (6) David, Samson (7) Judas (8) Ruth (9) Jonathan (10) Paul (with Peter)

Chapter 4

SERVING IN THE POWER OF GOD

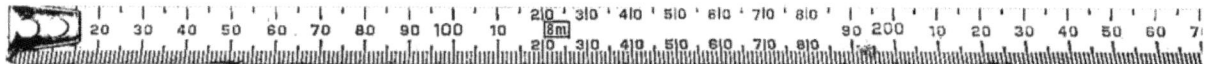

One of my (Alice) favorite stories is about a visit by one of my nephews. We don't live in the same state, but he came to visit me. He drove a very sporty Ferrari, and offered to let me drive it! I had never driven a sports car, but I was certainly willing to give it a try. As my nephew made himself comfortable on the front porch swing, I walked around behind the cute little car and began pushing it down the driveway. When I started to push it back *up* the hill, however, it wouldn't go more than a couple of feet before it started rolling back towards me. Naturally, I yelled for my nephew, who came running. "What's wrong, Aunt Alice? And ... *why* are you *pushing* the car?"

"Isn't that how you get it to go?" I asked him. He got into the car and told me to hop in. He turned the key in the ignition, the engine fired up – and off we went, up the hill! He said, "If you want to get it to go, you have to harness the power of the engine. Pretty simple, Alice. Really, pretty simple."

Now, before you write me off as Queen Ding-A-Ling of Sports Cars, you should know that the part about pushing the car didn't really happen. I've embellished the story in order to make a point. Wouldn't that be a ridiculous way to try to run our spiritual lives – trying to push them uphill, when necessary and plentiful power is available? Yet we do. We do so because we don't know how to tap into the power of the Holy Spirit who lives within us. Even though we know He is there, we falsely think that we have to use our own power to make progress in our spiritual lives.

Because so many of us don't know how to benefit from our real power source, the Holy Spirit, we will address the issue now. We suggest that you put aside any preconceived notions about running your own life, and focus on hearing what God might say to you as you read this chapter. He loves to reveal to us where we are running on soul-energy instead of Spirit-energy.

Power

*List two or three images that come to mind when you hear the word **power**:*

◯
◯
◯

Most of us have heard a sermon or a lesson based on Zechariah 4:6.
So he said to me, "This is the word of the Lord to Zerubbabel: **'Not by might nor by power, but by my Spirit,' says the Lord Almighty."**

It is very easy to agree with this verse, even if we don't know how to experience His power in our own lives. When we depend on our own power or might, we fail. We become discouraged and give up. So, what can we do to live as empowered believers, especially since we are expected to be strong spiritual leaders in our congregations?

*List 2 or 3 traits of a "**powerful leader**."*

◯
◯
◯

*List 2 or 3 things that come to mind when you hear the words, "**powerful church**."*

◯
◯
◯

Would you describe your church as a powerful church in the kingdom of God?
Explain why or why not:

POWER AS DEMONSTRATED IN THE OLD TESTAMENT

What do you think of when you hear the phrase "power as demonstrated in the Old Testament?"

Write down a few of your thoughts:

Does your list include such things as the creation, the flood, the crossing of the Red Sea, or the miracles performed by Elijah and Elisha? Remember when Elijah called down fire from heaven, or when he prayed that it wouldn't rain? How about the stories of David and Goliath, or the angel who slew hundreds of thousands of the enemy? Many Old Testament stories reveal the power of God at work. What about stories in the New Testament? Are there evidences of the power of God there as well? Which ones do you remember?

Does the list include any of these: the moving of the boulder that sealed Jesus' tomb; His resurrection and ascension; His healings and raising of the dead; the coming of the  Spirit at Pentecost; the transformation of the Apostle Paul from murderer to missionary? Did you include the transformation of Peter, the self-centered, Christ-denying disciple who later became the Spirit-filled preacher at Pentecost when thousands were converted? How about the power that people had to forgive those who stoned or imprisoned them? You can read about these and many more examples of the power of God in the pages of the Bible. One thing we can learn from all of them is the truth that all power is from God. Man is only a vessel through whom God works! How do we tap into this power? How do we become filled with the Holy Spirit so He can work through us?

Learning From Peter the Apostle

A church is unlikely to grow beyond the spiritual maturity of its leaders. Since churches are made up of people like you and me, *we* are a good place to begin! If we want the church to be empowered to serve the Lord, it has to begin with us.

There are many examples of individuals in the Bible who, weak in their own strength, learned how to be empowered beyond their own abilities. Someone most of us probably identify with is Peter. He seemed to embody so many of the traits that we all have. So, in our search for empowerment, let's take a closer look at his experience.

Things We Should NOT Think or Do

1. Do not think you are stronger than you really are.
With great confidence, Peter announced that he would never betray the Lord. He was in for a shock. This may be the hardest thing of all for us to accept: we really are weak! It seems to be programmed into us humans that "we can handle it." We laugh at toddlers when they want to do everything by themselves. While that is, indeed, how a toddler learns, God wants us to grow beyond the spiritual toddler phase.

Remember the story about the Ferrari? Our gifts and talents are like vehicles that God has given us for our work in the Kingdom. We have to mature before we get the driver's license. When we do, we must remember that we don't have to *push* the Ferrari! The power that mobilizes our gifts is the Holy Spirit. He is the "engine" of the spiritual life. A helpful, but humbling reminder: even Jesus said that He did nothing on His own! If the Son of God understood His dependence on the Father, shouldn't we look at spiritual life the same way?

2. Don't compare yourself with others.
Peter was adamant when he said, "Even if everyone else betrays you, I never will!" We know what happened soon after. This is a trap to avoid. Are you sure you're not guilty  of comparing yourself with others? Here's a good test: have you ever criticized those whose opinion differs from yours, or those who do something differently than the way you think it ought to be done? OF COURSE you have! It is built into our human DNA. How often do our thoughts sound something like, "Well, *I* know I'm right...I just wish that *you* knew it!" We see it manifested in our lives and in our congregations. Isn't this the root cause of most of our conflicts?

3. Don't speak before you think.
Peter certainly had a knack for breaking this principle! So do we. It's too easy to speak before we've taken time to think or pray about something. Learning to stop and think and pray will take a lot of practice for some. For others, the problem is NOT speaking up when they should. How often do people say they disagreed with a church vote, yet they didn't speak up?

Before opening our mouths, maybe we should practice asking Jesus if He approves of what we want to say, and open our *ears* to hear His answer first. We should search the Scriptures to see when Jesus commended or condemned people for their words. Jas 1:19 reminds us to be quick to listen and slow to speak or become angry. We have two ears and one mouth: a good reminder that we should listen twice as much as we speak!

4. Be aware of your weaknesses, and be slow to jump to conclusions about others.
We can get plenty of exercise by jumping to conclusions! We think we know why someone said something, what their motive was, and why their behavior wasn't such a good idea. When Jesus reminded His disciples to treat others as they wanted to be treated, He was giving us all an excellent rule of thumb. If we don't want to be misunderstood, criticized, or made fun of, then we shouldn't treat others in those ways. Do you want others to try to analyze your motives and jump to conclusions about you, hold a grudge against you, or gossip about you? Of course you don't, so you shouldn't do it, either.
"Do unto others" is a key lesson for empowered living.

5. Be careful that you are not challenging the authority of Jesus.
To do so would be to act as Satan's instrument. Surely, one of Peter's most embarrassing moments had to be Jesus' rebuke, "Get behind me, Satan!" Peter resisted what Jesus said would happen. Have you ever heard a church leader boldly declare, "Our church will *never* do that!" Or, have you heard the attitude expressed, "We've never done it that way before. Why change now?" On the other hand, change itself or new ways of doing things do not automatically mean the Spirit of God is leading in that direction. What works for one church may not be right for your church. What worked 50 years ago might not be the way the Spirit wants to do it today. The road to success is listening to what Jesus says; let Him direct the church!

BECOMING POWERFUL SERVANTS

Just as there are things we should be careful **not** to do, there are also things we **should be** doing. Through the years, Christians have often been known more for what they did *not* do than for what they *were* doing in the Kingdom. While we must know where we stand on moral and ethical issues, legalism is unappealing both to people and to God. The world is reeling with confusion over what is right and wrong, but the church isn't offering much direction. Our anchor has come loose, and we are afloat, too!

So, what *can* we do as leaders to be the empowered people that God can use to transform our church and community?

Consider the following suggestions as a good place to begin.

1. Be a leader who is determined to follow the Lord.
This is easier said than done, of course, but we must make an initial commitment to be  the kind of leader that Jesus can use. The initial commitment is just a beginning, however. Jesus reminded His disciples that commitment meant *daily* surrender to His Lordship and denial of self. Even though Peter got off track on a number of occasions because of his impetuosity, it is easy to see that he was committed to Jesus. When Jesus called him to lay down his fishing nets to become a fisher of men, Peter obeyed. Even when he denied that he knew Jesus, he was willing to repent and start over. He was no quitter and neither should we be, even when things become difficult.

2. Be willing to speak up to solve problems even when others are silent.
Do you find that it's usually just one or two on the deacon board who make the decisions – one or two who speak so strongly that anyone who disagrees (even if it's a majority) prefers to keep silent? Why? Fear, perhaps? A desire to be liked? Whatever the reason, it is tragic that they are too afraid to give voice to what they believe God is saying! God needs deacons who follow His leadership.

3. Be bold enough to follow Jesus even when it costs you something.
We are offended by politicians who are more concerned with their own reelections than they are about resolving important issues. But is that any worse than a deacon who remains silent or ignores the leading of the Spirit because he or she fears disapproval? How different might our deacon elections be, if the New Testament qualifications were

printed for all to see? We admire Stephen's faithfulness unto death, yet shrink back from the least bit of criticism that comes from a fellow church member. We need to boldly follow Jesus even when no one else understands what we are doing.

4. Be willing to repent when you fail the Lord.
There are no perfect people and there are no perfect deacons. The question is not **if** you will fail, but **when and how** you will fail the Lord. An attitude of humility in your role as deacon is essential. We **don't** know it all, even when we think we do! We don't always get it right. We don't always know what is best for our church or how to handle every situation. We will come closer to making wise decisions if we face up to this reality and get down on our knees to seek God's wisdom. When you make a mistake, ask for forgiveness!

5. Recognize your dependence upon the Spirit to serve in God's power.
"He came by it honestly," someone might say to explain another's actions. "His dad is just like that." Can we say the same thing about ourselves, that some traits we came by honestly from our parents? That is indeed true, but one thing we received that affects us more than our genes is the Adamic nature, the old sin nature we inherited because we are descendants of Adam and Eve. How does that nature manifest itself in our lives? The one characteristic that trips us up more frequently than any other is *independence*. We believe we can figure things out without God's help. It is difficult to admit to that attitude, but we can test ourselves by considering how often we pray before making a decision. If we do actually pray for God's will concerning a decision (rather than deciding on our own), how long do we wait and listen for His answer? What happens when we don't like what He says?

One of our main faults is trying to do things **for** Him instead of depending **on** Him. We make plans, but forget to pray. Or, we forget just who our teacher is, and hire consultants to help us with our decisions. We read secular books, forgetting that the Bible has truth for all situations. It isn't wrong, of course, to plan, hire consultants, or read other books, but prayer must be the foundation of everything.

6. Keep your focus on the Lord, and help others do the same.
Can you imagine throwing a birthday party for someone, inviting lots of guests, having lots of presents and food, and then forgetting to invite the guest of honor? Worse yet, you do invite the guest of honor, but then relegate that person to one lonely corner of the room while the rest of the crowd enjoys the party? Have you ever considered that God might sometimes feel like the uninvited or unwelcome guest at our church gatherings?

Ask yourself some pertinent questions:

(1) How much of what happens in your worship service honors Jesus?

(2) Is He the focus of your prayers, or is the focus on what you want from Him?

(3) When you listen to a sermon, do you learn more about who He is, or do you just get good tips for a happy life?

(4) In your deacons' or other planning meetings, do you talk about how to introduce others to Jesus, or do you worry about the budget?

(5) During the worship service prelude, do people enjoy each other's company or His company?

(6) Do the choir specials or other music make you want to applaud Jesus, or do you just applaud the choir and musicians?

(7) Have you asked Him what kind of music HE prefers in your services, or are you more concerned with pleasing the crowd?

It isn't as easy to stay focused on Jesus as you might think, but it is still imperative that you do so. Isn't that what the Christian life is all about? Can you imagine what church would look like, if every time we assembled, we were excited to share: (1) what Jesus did in our lives that week; (2) what Jesus taught us; and (3) what we plan to do for Jesus next week?

7. Don't quit when the going gets rough.

When discouraging things happen, people typically react in one of two ways: retreat or attack. What is your typical reaction when difficulties arise, especially at church? A lot of people leave and go to another church when conflicts erupt, not realizing that there simply aren't any problem-free institutions. Some will attack one another instead of attacking the problem! Others just quit trying. Instead of moving their membership, they take a back seat and distance themselves by inactivity or lack of attendance. When difficulties come to church, citizens of the Kingdom should marshal their resources and determine to be part of the solution!

8. Be willing to break tradition when the Lord asks you to do so.

Often, pastors and staff seem to hate the word *tradition*. Are they justified? Whether tradition is a good or a bad thing depends on the flexibility of the people. It isn't 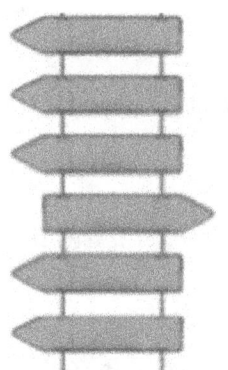 necessary to reinvent the wheel when it comes to how we do church. Some things that have worked well for many years *still* work well. Problems arise when people hold onto tradition so tightly that they won't even consider changes that would benefit the church. When tradition binds us as our taskmaster, it is bad. On the other hand, insisting on change simply for the sake of change, or insisting that change means throwing aside the wisdom of the ages, is also bad. Any of these abuses of tradition will devastate a church. A spiritual leader will follow God's advice about what to keep and what to change, even though these things are not always easy to discern. Change threatens almost everyone; so realize that change of any kind or degree will be at least temporarily disruptive. *Words of caution:* Be careful not to change the church just because the world is changing, and don't allow past traditions to keep you from making helpful changes. Sometimes churches don't know the difference between what is taught in the Bible and what is simply their tradition, such as insisting that worship be at 11:00 a.m.

9. Let your love for and praise of Jesus be evident and central in your life.

The Apostle Paul, in his letters to various churches, often mentioned their faith that was *spoken of throughout the whole world* (Rom 1:8). What is your church well known for? A strong youth group? A good ball team? A praise band? Impressive buildings? Conflicts and splits? Jesus said the world will know we are believers by the love we have one for another. Wouldn't it be wonderful if your community knew your church as a 'people who really love each other?' What a wonderful testimony it would be for your members to share with everyone, "If you need to be loved, come to our church. You'll learn about the One who loves you, and we'll love you, too!"

Scriptural Reminders Regarding the Power of God

In any discussion of God's power and our need to rely on it for our ministry, the Bible is our first and most important source of information.

Prayerfully study these verses and comments, asking the Lord to speak to your heart.

1. The source of our power is the Holy Spirit.
But you will receive power when the Holy Spirit comes on you; and you will be my witnesses in Jerusalem, and in all Judea and Samaria, and to the ends of the earth (Acts 1:8). If we try to "do church" in our own strength, we will fail. Our Sunday meeting and greeting may continue, but power to reach the lost or revive believers will cease. Why? Because we are weak! We must rely on God to release His power in and through us. Paul pleaded with God to take away the thorn in his flesh. Like Paul, we sometimes ask for our problems to be removed. God would advise us as He advised Paul, "My grace is sufficient for you" (2 Cor 12:9). Listen to the rest of that passage. God also says to Paul, "My power, my strength, is made perfect in your weakness." Paul understood that God's power was more important than the removal of his thorn, and responded, "Therefore most gladly I will rather boast in my infirmities, that the power of Christ may rest upon me!" Our weaknesses are God's opportunities. Let's quit trying to do His work without His power.

God's power is available; we must learn how to yield to His power within us. Where do we start? The first step is to realize we can't do His work without Him! As long as we keep trying, He will keep waiting. Why are our churches weak and powerless? Perhaps it is because God is still waiting for us to put our faith in Him rather than in ourselves.

2. Our responsibility is to cooperate with the power that is within us.
He is the one we proclaim, admonishing and teaching everyone with all wisdom, so that we may present everyone fully mature in Christ. To this end I strenuously contend with all the energy Christ so powerfully works in me (Col 1:28-29). If you study these verses more closely, you will see that the **goals and methods** of our ministry should be: (1) **to proclaim Jesus;** (2) **to admonish (warn) and teach everyone with all wisdom;** (3) **to present everyone fully mature in Christ;** and (4) **to work *with* the energy Christ so powerfully works in me.** Do you ever wonder why so many books have been written about successful church leadership, when Paul has told us what we need to know in these two verses? Our churches would be different places if we followed his advice!

Take time to think about and answer the following questions:

a. Where is your church strong in the 4 areas Paul mentioned?

b. What are your leaders specifically doing to carry out Paul's instructions?

> 1. Proclaiming Jesus
> 2. Warning and teaching with all wisdom
> 3. Presenting everyone mature in Christ
> 4. Working with Christ's energy in us

c. Where are they failing to do as well as they could do?

d. What can they do to become stronger in these areas of life and ministry?

3. We must refrain from grieving or quenching the Spirit, our source of power.
And do not grieve the Holy Spirit of God, with whom you were sealed for the day of redemption (Eph 4:30). *Do not quench the Spirit* (1 Thess 5:19). Most believers cannot fathom that they might be grieving (saddening) or quenching the Spirit (keeping Him from doing His work). But we do grieve and quench Him. All of us do. We do it both individually and corporately. In this life, we will never completely stop doing so, but we can make progress.

Where do we begin? Well, first of all, we must realize that we *do* regularly quench and grieve God's Spirit. Next, we must learn what grieves and quenches Him. We should know what to do when we do grieve or quench Him. We must make a definite commitment to stop doing it. Finally – and continually – we must ask for His help.

Look back over the tips given above as you answer the following questions:

a. Where do you need work so that you, personally, will stop grieving or quenching the Spirit?

b. How does your church grieve or quench the Spirit?

c. Will you, as a leader in your church, ask for God's help and make a definite commitment to allow Him to show you where you are failing in the above areas? Will you allow Him to do something about what He reveals to you?

Bow in prayer and make that commitment to Him now.

Whenever a Christian realizes how easily and regularly he/she grieves the Spirit, and has a genuine desire to stop doing so, God will ensure that progress happens. He is faithful to reveal where we are grieving Him. He is faithful to cleanse and restore us to fellowship with Himself when we confess and ask Him to forgive us. But if we continue to rationalize our sin, we will make little or no progress. God simply will not empower a sinful vessel. He demands clean vessels, committed vessels, surrendered and pliable vessels; He never will bless disobedience.

He is willing to open our eyes to see His holiness and to understand how we must live in harmony with Him and His will, if we ask Him and yield to Him. Nothing grieves Him more than to see His children suffer needlessly and serve without power. But He will never force us to commit to His Lordship and indwelling power. We must make the choice, and when we do, He will move heaven and earth to bless us and our churches.

4. The prayers of a righteous person make tremendous power available.
Therefore confess your sins to each other and pray for each other so that you may be healed. The prayer of a righteous person is powerful and effective (Jas 5:16). The Amplified Version of this verse gives additional insight: *Confess to one another therefore your faults (your slips, your false steps, your offenses, your sins) and pray [also] for one another, that you may be healed and restored [to a spiritual tone of mind and heart]. The earnest (heartfelt, continued) prayer of a righteous man makes tremendous power available [dynamic in its working]* (Amplified Bible, James 5:16).

Note some of the details of this verse. Confession results in restoration to a spiritual tone of mind and heart. The result of that is the ability to pray powerful prayers that release the power of God in our midst. The power available is **dynamic in its working.** When we learn how to pray correctly, when we are cleansed and available, God is able to work in our lives and in our churches in freedom and power. If and when we meet the requirements, He does the rest!

5. We serve, not by our own ability and effort, but in the Spirit's power.
For I resolved to know nothing while I was with you except Jesus Christ and him crucified. I came to you in weakness with great fear and trembling. My message and my preaching were not with wise and persuasive words, but with a demonstration of the Spirit's power, so that your faith might not rest on human wisdom, but on God's power (NIV, 1 Corinthians 2:3-5). God will never share His glory with another. Most of us think we are depending on God, but often we are really depending on ourselves. When is the last time something happened in your church that could only be explained as the power of God?

Most people who read about Paul or study his letters would never describe him as a weak and powerless individual. Yet, he describes himself as one who has learned that he is only powerful when he realizes his own weakness and dependence upon the Spirit. Have you learned this lesson? Or are you still trying to solve problems in your own wisdom? God's divine power has already given us everything we need to have power in our church. What is short-circuiting His power in your church?

6. God is able to do more than we can ask or imagine by His power in us.
Now to him who is able to do immeasurably more than all we can ask or imagine, according to his power that is at work within us, to him be glory in the church and in Christ Jesus throughout all generations, for ever and ever! Amen (Eph 3:20-21). Has your church stopped dreaming big dreams? Are you struggling just to maintain the status quo? Are you reaching your community with the message of Jesus' love? Is your church 'aging out,' the older members dying off and the younger folks not coming? Do your members tithe? Is your congregation mission-minded? Is there a spirit of depression among those who are holding on and hoping that your church won't have to close its doors in a few years? Does Eph 3:20-21 describe the attitude of your church? Can your church in its present existence be described as powerful? If not, why not? If God can indeed do more than we can ask or imagine by the power that is within us, then why aren't we experiencing such power? This is a question you and your fellow deacons and staff should ask prayerfully, seeking God's answers.

7. God has already given us everything we need for life and godliness.
His divine power has given us everything we need for a godly life through our knowledge of him who called us by his own glory and goodness. Through these he has given us his very great and precious promises, so that through them you may participate in the divine nature, having escaped the corruption in the world caused by evil desires (2 Pet 1:2-4). If we already have everything we need for life and godliness, why is it often absent from our lives? If we have the Spirit and His power and everything we need to live life, why is it not benefiting us? Our conclusion must be that we either (1) don't believe we have it, (2) don't know what to do with it, or we (3) aren't humble enough to obey the instructions. Which is it with you and your church?

UNDERSTANDING SPIRITUAL BURNOUT

Recently, I (Alice) saw my very first episode of Survivor. One team's members had dwindled down to two, and one of the two was going to be eliminated that night. When  the host interviewed them, both said they had learned the importance of FIRE. Out in the wild, no fire means no heat, no cooking, no hot water, no protection from wild animals, and so on. One told how his carelessness had let the fire go out once, and how it had taken over two hours to start another one.

At the closing ceremony, the contestant who had been eliminated had to snuff out his torch before leaving the group, and the competition - for good. I was surprised how the snuffing out of his torch affected me! It reminds me of how we, too, suffer when our *spiritual fires* are extinguished.

In Lev 6:13, the Lord told Moses to be sure that Aaron (the priest) and his sons knew the following command: *"The fire must be kept burning on the altar continuously; it must not go out."* The Lord emphasized that this was a command (i.e., *not a suggestion*). We know this because it was repeated three times in six verses!

The ones responsible for keeping the fire burning were the priests - those who were in charge of worship. Perhaps a New Testament counterpart of this command is Rom 12:11. *"Never lack in zeal and in earnest endeavor; be aglow and burning with the Spirit, serving the Lord"* (Amplified Bible, Romans 12:11). We can agree that God expects His children to keep the fire burning in their lives and in the church. We can also agree that we are not always successful. If this is important to the Lord, it must be important to us, too, so let's explore further by answering the following questions: *(1) What causes the spiritual fire to dim or go out in our lives and churches; and, (2) What can we do to keep the fire burning or to rekindle it?*

What Causes the Spiritual Fire to Go Out or Diminish?

According to Webster's dictionary, *burnout* is defined as *fatigue, frustration, or apathy resulting from prolonged stress, overwork, or intense activity.* Those who serve as leaders in churches are susceptible to burn out. Why? Because most leaders, at least at first, are idealistic and want to do a good job. This is certainly true for newly ordained deacons. What a humbling experience to be selected and ordained for the Lord's service! Unfortunately, the new deacon may become quickly disillusioned with both their position and their congregation. Why? Because deacons are often expected to: solve *all* of the problems; keep the church and its programs moving forward; work with the staff in ministry to the flock; and keep the church financially stable, just to mention a few!

Another factor is a tendency to forget that one's spiritual health is easily compromised by criticism. Any deacon who attempts to plan and make decisions without the foundations of prayer and Bible study is in grave danger of letting his fire go out! One's spiritual fire must be strong for effective, grace-filled ministry.

What Does Spiritual Burnout Look Like?

It isn't always easy to see yourself or others as being on the verge of burnout. Some of us are able to smile and go through the motions of the spiritual life even when we are miserable! Eventually, however, burnout will become obvious. What traits indicate the downward spiral of spiritual burnout?

Evaluate your own life by these criteria:

How often do you have these feelings/thoughts?	Never	Rarely	Sometimes	Often
	1	2	3	4
1. Ministry is simply a task, something to be done, but with no real joy in doing it.	1	2	3	4
2. The desire to do just enough to get by, but not with enthusiasm.	1	2	3	4
3. A feeling of being overwhelmed with the responsibility of the position.	1	2	3	4
4. Disengagement; being present, but not really being there.	1	2	3	4
5. A loss of ideals or hope; depression.	1	2	3	4
6. A sense of helplessness and pessimism.	1	2	3	4
7. Feelings of failure and loss of perspective; apathy.	1	2	3	4
8. Not feeling satisfied about the work done.	1	2	3	4
9. Feeling useless, low self-esteem.	1	2	3	4
10. Cynical and negative about others and the work.	1	2	3	4
11. Easily angered, having a short fuse.	1	2	3	4
12. Tired of hearing what other people think.	1	2	3	4

Evaluating your score: How did you do? Did you notice any of these tendencies in yourself or others? If you see danger signs in others, share your concerns in a spirit of love and godly concern. Any statement(s) you ranked as "4" should be addressed immediately, with rankings of "3" close behind, because early signs of burnout are often intermittent, cropping up only occasionally at first and increasing over time.

Taking Another Look

Rate yourself on these questions.

How often do you have these feelings/thoughts?	Never	Rarely	Sometimes	Often
	1	2	3	4
1. I feel I often cannot solve the problems presented to me.	1	2	3	4
2. I feel I have little influence on decisions that are made.	1	2	3	4
3. I am unclear about the duties of my ministry.	1	2	3	4
4. I feel I am not trained for the role I am in.	1	2	3	4
5. I think that other people who are serving with me are as unclear about the ministry as I am.	1	2	3	4
6. I often find myself caught in the middle of conflict.	1	2	3	4
7. I am confused about the overall purpose of my role.	1	2	3	4
8. I see hypocrisy among those with whom I serve.	1	2	3	4
9. People who serve with me are in competition with each other.	1	2	3	4
10. Church politics and power struggles discourage me.	1	2	3	4
11. Church responsibilities interfere with my personal life.	1	2	3	4
12. I don't have time to handle what's expected of me.	1	2	3	4
13. I rarely feel qualified to do the work expected of me.	1	2	3	4
14. I feel that the majority of my time is spent on what I call non-essentials.	1	2	3	4
15. I feel like I do too much administrative work and not enough 'hands-on' ministry.	1	2	3	4
16. I receive little or no feedback from the staff and other leaders as to how I am doing.	1	2	3	4
17. I don't feel as if my suggestions are taken seriously.	1	2	3	4
18. I don't feel as if I am making much of a difference in the work of my church.	1	2	3	4

Evaluating your score: How did you do? Remember, rankings of "4" require your immediate attention, with rankings of "3" following close behind. You may need wise counsel to help you assess the situation. Get it! Avoid burnout! It is never God's will for His servant's fire to be snuffed out. The ministry of the deacon *is* important for the health and growth of your church, but your ministry as a deacon is *not* as important as your spiritual health.

WHY IS MINISTRY BURNOUT SO PREVALENT?

Increasing numbers of churches are having difficulty finding people willing to serve as deacons...or in any other leadership position, for that matter. What's behind this alarming trend? Why are people reluctant to serve the Lord, especially in the role of deacon?

Consider some of the following possibilities:

1. "Ministry" is never really finished. There's always another thing waiting.

2. It's hard to tell if your ministry is having any positive results, even though you work hard at it.

3. Some parts of ministry are repetitive and can become boring.

4. People have varying opinions and expectations as to what you should be doing, and they are not hesitant to tell you so! Criticism and lack of appreciation contribute to discouragement and burnout.

5. The constant emotional and physical drain on leaders contributes to fatigue.

6. Role expectations tempt deacons to think they have to be all things to all people. When church members expect every leader to have all of the abilities and competencies they personally need, the conscientious deacon may attempt to work outside of his gifts/abilities, placing him/her at risk for burnout.

7. A leader who tries, but fails, is a candidate for discouragement and burnout.

Avoiding Spiritual Burnout

One of the best ways to avoid burnout is to realize that it can happen to anyone! When you think you're not vulnerable is when you are at the greatest risk. Many newly ordained deacons don't realize what pressures they will face. While most begin their service optimistically, few are prepared for how quickly their perspectives can change.

Some of the following suggestions may help you avoid burnout.

1. Have an accountability partner; one who will help you watch for signs of burnout in your life, even as you help them keep watch over their own lives.

2. Become familiar with the causes and symptoms of burnout so you can avoid the causes and recognize the symptoms.

3. Keep your spiritual disciplines strong. Bible study, prayer, and worship in particular will help you avoid burnout. Never give out more than you take in!

4. Remember to confess your sins the moment you are convicted. Nothing quenches the Spirit of God more quickly than unconfessed sin.

5. Rely on the Spirit for all of life, not just your church service.

6. Discover your Spirit-given gifts as well as your natural abilities, and work out of those. Don't say *yes* to other ministries just because someone asked or because no one else is willing. Working outside of your gifts is a good way to burn out.

7. Keep yourself physically and emotionally healthy since not doing so can contribute to spiritual problems.

8. Don't try to do work that only the Holy Spirit can do. Don't try to fix people or solve church problems with your own wisdom. When your solutions don't work, you may feel guilty or discouraged about failing, which can lead to burnout.

9. Whenever you begin to feel a lack of interest or enthusiasm about serving the Lord, take time to draw aside in prayer, worship and confession. Admit to the Lord what you are experiencing, and ask for His help. Catch the problem before it gets out of hand. Share with your accountability partner(s) so they can pray for you, encourage you, and offer objective advice and insight.

10. Don't ever give in to the temptation to do just enough to get by, or simply to go through the motions. Dig deep and find out why you are tempted to do only enough to get by in ministry.

11. Don't make excuses if your fire - your enthusiasm for the Lord - is burning low. Try to find the problem, and deal with it. Wishful thinking (wishing you were more spiritual) will never overcome spiritual apathy.

12. Don't take on ministries or try to solve problems that aren't your responsibility. A person who has a servant's heart has to learn how to say "No."

13. Watch out for others who may be showing signs of burnout. Reach out to them. This is a good way to keep an eye on yourself, too. After all, who wants advice from somebody who doesn't practice what they preach?

14. Don't let others' feedback about your ministry be the final word on how you are doing. Serve as unto the Lord! Ask Him how you are doing. Sometimes praise or criticism from others sidetracks us into disillusionment or even boastfulness.

15. Avoid the *monotony syndrome*, always doing the same thing in the same way. Change may be difficult, but it can also be a source of revitalization. Learning how to think outside the box can keep us from boredom and burnout.

Avoiding spiritual burnout seems to be a topic that church leaders neglect, for some reason. You should make it a top priority in your life and service. It is much easier to prevent burnout than it is to cure it once it hits. Revisit these pages regularly as a way to refresh your memory on the topic and keep you alert. Self-care and spiritual growth are not optional if you want to accomplish what God has in store for you in this ministry. As you read God's word and remain alert to what is happening in your life and church, you will realize just how many of God's servants have faced the very same things you are facing.

Section Two:

Improving the Spiritual Health of Your Church

5. ASSESSING THE SPIRITUAL HEALTH OF YOUR CHURCH 97

6. MEETING REQUIREMENTS FOR EFFECTIVE CHURCH MINISTRY 111

7. FOLLOWING JESUS, THE HEAD OF THE CHURCH 129

8. KNOWING AND DOING GOD'S WILL 153

Chapter 5

Assessing the Spiritual Health of Your Church

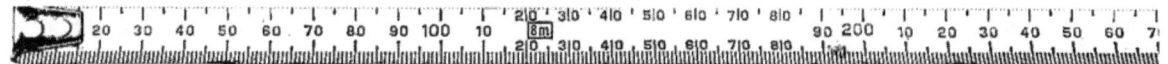

What Makes a Church Healthy?

One of the first questions a deacon should ask is, "How spiritually healthy is my church?" We *want* the church to be healthy, but often we don't know how to measure its health, much less what to do to improve its health. In the final analysis, the spiritual health of a congregation is determined by the spiritual health of its individual members. But it is helpful to have an idea of the overall health of the entire congregation. While there are not any specific, scientific methods for determining spiritual health, there are indicators. Take a few moments to complete the following assessment.

My Personal Assessment of My Congregation

From your own observation and knowledge of the people in your congregation, how you would rate your church in the following areas:

	Low				High
1. Members know and use their spiritual gifts.	1	2	3	4	5
2. The attendance of our Sunday School is increasing.	1	2	3	4	5
3. A majority of our members read their Bibles daily and pray.	1	2	3	4	5
4. We have an organized approach to witnessing to the lost.	1	2	3	4	5

5. We are baptizing adults as well as children on a regular basis. 1 2 3 4 5

6. Our budget reflects a strong emphasis on:
    a. supporting our church's ministries to our own members 1 2 3 4 5
    b. home and foreign missions 1 2 3 4 5
    c. creative outreach ministries to our own community 1 2 3 4 5
    d. helping the poor in our community 1 2 3 4 5

7. We have a strong ministry to the elderly and widowed members. 1 2 3 4 5

8. We have a good number of our members who go on mission trips or minister in our community to non-members. 1 2 3 4 5

9. We are organized to meet the needs of our own members:
    a. grief support 1 2 3 4 5
    b. hospitalized and shut-ins 1 2 3 4 5
    c. financial difficulties 1 2 3 4 5
    d. marital/family problems 1 2 3 4 5

10. Our worship service is designed both to meet members' needs and to appeal to visitors/seekers/the unsaved. 1 2 3 4 5

11. Prayer meeting is well attended and effective. 1 2 3 4 5

12. There is a strong emphasis on Bible study and prayer in all aspects of our church's programs. 1 2 3 4 5

13. At least 75% of our members seem to be diligently working at becoming better disciples of Jesus. 1 2 3 4 5

14. A large number of our members tithe. 1 2 3 4 5

15. Our church has a good reputation in the community. 1 2 3 4 5

16. Our church regularly sponsors programs that help members know each other on more than a superficial basis. 1 2 3 4 5

17. There is an obvious spirit of unity in our church. 1 2 3 4 5

18. Outsiders would call us a friendly, caring, and accepting church. 1 2 3 4 5

19. We are making a special effort to disciple our youth and children. 1 2 3 4 5

20. We work at making all races, classes, and cultures feel welcome and comfortable at our church. 1 2 3 4 5

21. Praying for the lost is a strong emphasis in our prayer meetings. 1 2 3 4 5

22. The Lordship of Christ and the empowerment of God's Spirit are the main focus of all that we do. 1 2 3 4 5

23. Our worship services could be described as Spirit-filled and God-honoring. 1 2 3 4 5

24. One of our major emphases is teaching people how to worship. 1 2 3 4 5

25. Our church is good at assimilating new members and helping them feel they are part of the congregation. 1 2 3 4 5

EVALUATING YOUR ASSESSMENT

1. Note the questions that received the highest ratings. What is your church presently doing that makes it strong in that particular area? What can you do to make it even stronger?

2. Note the questions that received the lowest ratings. Why is your church weak in those particular areas? How can you strengthen these areas?

3. Decide on at least one specific thing to do in the highest and lowest areas this coming year. Write them down.

4. Discuss your ideas with other deacons and staff members.

A major reason for the failure of churches to grow spiritually is that they do not have a good balance. When a church focuses more on maintenance - *keeping things running smoothly* - than it does on mission - *following where God is leading* – it gets out of balance. Two analogies can help us understand this concept. First, picture a merry-go-round. As long as everything looks nice and the motor keeps running, a merry-go-round is in good shape. It never really goes anywhere, but the people who ride it are happy. Sometimes new people jump on, and sometimes people jump off. As long as the merry-go-round keeps going around, it is no cause for concern. Can you picture your church as a merry-go-round? We never really go anywhere, but as long as everything looks nice and the engine keeps running, everyone's happy. People come and go; staff members come and go. Finances go up and come back down. The seasons go by, the years go by, round and round, each one looking like the last. We're not really going anywhere, but we're happy.

Now, picture a cruise ship. A cruise ship needs great food and great entertainment, along with great staff to take great care of the passengers. Cruise ships *cruise;* it's what they do. Passengers pay their fees to travel in luxury. If the food isn't up to par, a new chef is hired. If the crew doesn't please the passengers, new crews are hired. It's all about leisure. Can you picture your church as a cruise ship? If the passengers are happy, we consider ourselves to be in good shape. We seem to be more comfortable staying tied to the *dock of tradition.* We may take a short trip around the harbor occasionally, but we expect to return to the dock in a timely fashion. Few new passengers come aboard, and when the passengers become restless, we usually get a new crew and a new chef, and then we're happy again.

Would you be offended if someone described your church using either of those analogies? Can you be objective about your church? Would you want to know if your church is caught up in a meaningless, pointless cycle? Talk with your fellow deacons; take an objective look at your church. Ask these questions: "How balanced is our ministry?" "Where is our focus?"

Where is Your Church's Focus?

Place an "X" on the line to indicate where you think your church is presently focused.

1. Focused on ourselves   vs.   Focused on God

_____

2. Concerned with how we feel/think   vs.   Concerned how God feels/thinks

_____

3. That WE be blessed   vs.   That HE be pleased

_____

4. That we receive FROM Him   vs.   That we give TO Him

_____

5. That WE be in control   vs.   That we submit to HIS control

_____

6. That God and others see our perspective   vs.   That we see from God's perspective

_____

7. We fight with each other   vs.   We fight spiritually against principalities and powers

_____

8. We expect people to come to our church   vs.   We focus on going out where the people are

_____

9. We demand our own way   vs.   We seek the will of God above all else

_____

10. We want to get something out of worship   vs.   We want God to be pleased with our worship

_____

11. We criticize and complain when things do not go our way	vs.	We are so busy praising God, we do not complain or criticize
12. We rationalize our sins and shortcomings	vs.	We repent of our sins and ask God's help to overcome them
13. We want to worship and serve as we prefer	vs.	We seek God's preferences for our worship and service
14. We compare ourselves with other churches	vs.	We ask the Lord to examine us and change us into His image
15. We know what is best for our church	vs.	We humbly ask God to show us His will for our church

Evaluation

Examine where you have marked the scales, and note the areas in which your church seems to be unbalanced.

What areas of weakness stood out in your mind as you completed this inventory?

What are some ways you can build on your strengths or overcome your weaknesses as a church?

The Balance Between Maintenance and Mission

Leaders can gauge the spiritual health of their congregation by assessing the church's main emphases and programs. Is the church more focused on **maintenance** (keeping the church afloat and its members satisfied) or **mission**  (reaching out to the community, both local and worldwide)? The ideal answer, of course, is that the church is well balanced between the two! Both mission and maintenance are church endeavors mandated by God. Neglect of either emphasis will put us out of balance and into difficulty. Overemphasize *mission,* and you risk members burning out and dropping out because they are overworked or neglecting their own needs. Overemphasize *maintenance,* and you fail to obey the Great Commission with the risk of becoming like the Dead Sea: all intake, no outflow. So, the question to ask is, "How can we maintain a good balance?" Does the Bible give us any insight at all?

Let's look first at what it teaches us about an emphasis on **maintenance**:

1. We must keep the flock healthy spiritually.
Keep watch over yourselves and all the flock of which the Holy Spirit has made you overseers. Be shepherds of the church of God, which he bought with his own blood. I know that after I leave, savage wolves will come in among you and will not spare the flock. Even from your own number men will arise and distort the truth in order to draw away disciples after them. So be on your guard! Remember that for three years I never stopped warning each of you night and day with tears (Acts 20:28-31).

2. We must train people how to minister to themselves and to others. We need more practice in building each other up in the Lord!
We who are strong ought to bear with the failings of the weak and not to please ourselves. Each of us should please our neighbors for their good, to build them up (Rom 15:1-2).

3. We must help our members discover and use their spiritual gifts.
But to each one of us grace has been given as Christ apportioned it. So Christ himself gave the apostles, the prophets, the evangelists, the pastors and teachers, to equip his people for works of service, so that the body of Christ may be built up until we all reach unity in the faith and in the knowledge of the Son of God and become mature, attaining to the whole measure of the fullness of Christ.

Then we will no longer be infants, tossed back and forth by the waves, and blown here and there by every wind of teaching and by the cunning and craftiness of people in their deceitful scheming. Instead, speaking the truth in love, we will grow to become in every respect the mature body of him who is the head, that is, Christ. From him the whole body, joined and held together by every supporting ligament, grows and builds itself up in love, as each part does its work (Eph 4:7, 11-16).

4. Empowerment must come before mission can be effective.
On one occasion, while he was eating with them, he gave them this command: "Do not leave Jerusalem, but wait for the gift my Father promised, which you have heard me speak about. For John baptized with water, but in a few days you will be baptized with the Holy Spirit."
Then they gathered around him and asked him, "Lord, are you at this time going to restore the kingdom to Israel?"

He said to them: "It is not for you to know the times or dates the Father has set by his own authority. But you will receive power when the Holy Spirit comes on you; and you will be my witnesses in Jerusalem, and in all Judea and Samaria, and to the ends of the earth" (Acts 1:4-8).

Now, what about **mission**? How can we get our members involved in reaching outside the walls of our church? Mission usually results from healthy maintenance. A healthy church will draw people to it, and spiritually healthy people are more likely to follow the Lord's command to reach the lost world with the gospel.

The Biblical instruction for **mission** is clearly spelled out in Mt 28:19-20. We are to **go, teach, baptize, and disciple** people. There are hundreds of ways to fulfill this command. How are you doing with this balance *in your own life*: are you reaching out to others as well as caring for your own needs? How is *your church* doing with this balance between maintenance and mission?

MAINTAINING A GOOD BALANCE

How can you help your church maintain a good balance between maintenance and mission?

1. Start with yourself.
God has led you to a position of leadership. Anytime you want to help your church, you must understand that it always begins with *you*. Where are *you* out of balance? How can *you* restore the balance between maintenance and mission in *your* life?

2. Help by teaching and training.
Your congregation looks to its leaders to help them grow in their spiritual lives. Use your own spiritual gifts in as many ways as possible to equip others in your congregation. Has your church had a study on how to find and develop spiritual gifts? That would be a great place to begin!

3. Study the letters to the seven churches in the book of Revelation to learn what the Lord said about their strengths/weaknesses. (See the next section.)

4. Pray!
Because we know God desires this balance, we can be assured of His help. We may be aware of our problems, but not know the remedy. God knows both the problems and their solutions, and is more than willing to help your church. Don't forget to pray!

WINNING JESUS' APPROVAL

She was ecstatic, and wanted everyone to know why. "I got an A+ on one of Dr. C's assignments!" she exclaimed, "I've been trying for two years!"

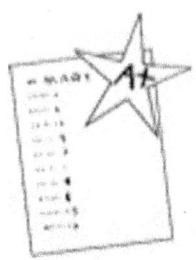

Most of us have had our efforts affirmed or rewarded at one time or another. Jesus' statement that the good steward will one day hear him say, "Well done, you good and faithful servant!" encourages us to remain faithful. Hearing those words *one day* is surely a worthy goal, but have you considered that we should be receiving His words of commendation *now*? The church should also be hearing the same "Well done!" with regard to its work and ministry.

Do you think there is any basis for believing that the Lord wants to commend His churches today, that He is concerned about their work and ministry in the world? The best way to answer this question is to study the letters to the seven churches in the Book of the Revelation. While it is easy to get lost in the mysteries of this fascinating book of the Bible, we must focus on the fact that Jesus IS concerned with how His churches are faring in the world. He WILL always let us know what He thinks about us, if we will ask Him and listen to His reply.

Jesus' Assessment of His churches
(The Book of the Revelation, chapters 2-3)

Prayerfully read the following summation of the letters to the seven churches. (You will also want to read the letters in their entirety.)

Examine carefully what Jesus said to His churches, asking the Spirit to speak to you about your own church.

Underline the phrases that seem to stand out as descriptions of your church.

Words of **Commendation:**
1. Hard work and perseverance.
2. Cannot tolerate wicked people.
3. Perseverance and enduring hardship for Jesus' name.
4. Have not grown weary in their work and service.
5. Hate the practices of false teachers.
6. Remain true to Jesus' name in the midst of wicked surroundings.
7. Do not renounce faith in Jesus during persecution.
8. Full of love, faith, service, and perseverance.
9. Busy doing kingdom work.
10. Have kept God's word and not denied Jesus' name.
11. Have kept God's command to endure patiently.

Words of **Condemnation:**
1. Have forsaken your First Love (Jesus).
2. Tolerating false teaching.
3. Do not hold strong leaders accountable (Jezebel).
4. Deeds are not complete in the sight of God.
5. Are lukewarm.
6. Proud and boastful about finances.
7. Unaware of own condition: wretched, pitiful, poor, blind, and naked.

WORDS OF **ADVICE:**
  1. Remember and repent.
  2. Do the things you did at first.
  3. Be faithful.
  4. Hold onto what you have until I come.
  5. Wake up!
  6. Strengthen what remains and is about to die.
  7. Remember what you have received and heard: obey it and repent.
  8. Hold onto what you have, so that no one will take your crown.
  9. Come to me for what you really need.
10. Be earnest and repent.

WORDS OF **WARNING:**
1. If you don't repent, I will come to you and remove your lampstand from its place.
2. If you don't repent, I will soon come to you and fight against you.
3. I will repay each according to his deeds.
4. If you don't repent, I will come like a thief.
5. I will spit you out of my mouth.
6. I will rebuke and discipline you.

WORDS OF **PROMISE:**
  1. I will keep you from the hour of trial that is going to come upon the whole world to test those who live on the earth.
  2. I will make you a pillar in the temple of God.
  3. If you hear My knock and open the door, I will enter in and fellowship with you.
  4. I will give the right to sit with Me on My throne.
  5. If you overcome, you will eat from the tree of life in the paradise of God.
  6. I will give you the crown of life.
  7. You will not be hurt by the second death.
  8. If you overcome, you can eat of the hidden manna.
  9. I will not impose any other burden on the faithful.
10. To him who overcomes and does My will to the end, I will give authority over the nations.
11. The worthy will walk with Me dressed in white; his name will not be blotted from the book of life.
12. I will acknowledge you before the Father and his angels.

Encourage the other members of your deacon group and the staff to record their own impressions as they read these messages. Talk with each other about what God might be saying to your church. Discuss what your church can do to heed any warnings. Decide how best to follow the advice Jesus shared with His servant, John.

Do you ever notice the certificates of ratings that are prominently posted in every restaurant? This is important information, though not everyone takes notice. It may be that we do see when a restaurant has a low rating, but we don't know why. If the rating is low because the refrigerator was not quite cold enough, that is one thing. But it is quite another problem if the restaurant was cited because the inspector found mouse droppings in the food! Wouldn't that influence you the next time you thought about eating there?

What might happen if our churches were required to prominently post a rating scale? Not the rating we would give ourselves, but the Lord's evaluation. Would a low rating have any influence on the members, or on prospective members? Maybe it would depend on the reason for the low rating. If our low rating was posted for all to see, would we work hard to bring up our score? Probably so!

The Challenge

Once we evaluate where we are and where we want to be, there are steps to take. There is a process to follow in order to become what God desires. A good place to begin is with these four steps:

1. **Examine our own spiritual lives. Are we walking closely with God?**
2. **Seek God's vision for our church.**
3. **Develop a strategy to bring that vision to fruition.**
4. **Implement the strategy.**

At a training conference in Atlanta, I (Keith) heard one of the leaders say that the first two steps are easier than the last two. "Most of us want to grow spiritually," he said, "and maybe we're even comfortable developing the plans for our church. "But," he said, "the last two steps are the most difficult," because the work always slows down at the point of strategy. Implementing the vision - deciding what to change and how to bring about that change - is no easy task! When the pursuit of a vision comes to a standstill, the roadblock is usually at the point of implementation.

This same issue came up at a deacons' retreat, when the oldest deacon in the room said, "Keith, before we start, I'd like to ask your advice. I've been a deacon for years, and I love my church. Our problem is getting things done. When the deacons bring an idea before the church for a vote, and the church approves it, well … that's when we have a problem. We never seem to follow through! Can you give us some suggestions on how to get our church to follow through?" The problem is more common than you might think. Failure at the point of implementation often plagues our churches. The power of God is critical here, because if a church cannot implement its vision, it surely cannot be effective in Kingdom work.

A Truth to Remember

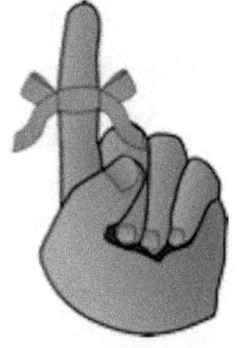

It is important to keep in mind that many little things can be just as detrimental to the health of your church body as one or two major issues. In Jonathan Swift's Gulliver's Travels[8], the mental image of Gulliver being tied down by tiny people who were only 1/12th his size can help keep us on the lookout for the many tiny things that can become huge if not dealt with successfully. Hurt feelings, neglected members, impatient words, etc., in themselves may seem small. When they accumulate, however, over a period of years, the result can be disastrous!

Are you flexible? Is your church? *Change* is usually an unwelcome word, but our churches need to be continually made new in order to be a blessing to a constantly changing world. When is the last time you saw the Lord do something in your church that could only be explained as the work of God?

The Acts 1:8 Challenge

But you will receive power when the Holy Spirit comes on you; and you will be my witnesses in Jerusalem, and in all Judea and Samaria, and to the ends of the earth (Acts 1:8).

Jesus instructed the disciples to be empowered by the Spirit before reaching out to the world. Are you empowered? Is that how you would describe your church?

He also commanded them to go *first* to Jerusalem. How would you describe your church's *Jerusalem*? For the disciples, *Jerusalem* was right where they were. This is also true for us: *Jerusalem is right where we are.* Do you know who lives within a five-mile radius of your church? That is your *Jerusalem*. Have you conducted a survey or done a demographic study to learn about your Jerusalem? It can be eye opening. One local church was shocked to discover that there was an area of extreme poverty in their

---

[8] Swift, Jonathan, Gulliver's Travels, gutenberg.org.

Jerusalem. They reached out to be Christ's witnesses there. Their initial outreach failed, however, due to poor planning. They had planned for meeting the community's needs for food and clothing, but they had not planned for meeting the community's spiritual needs. The result was that there were no converts, no disciples made.

What about your *Judea* and your *Samaria*? Your *Judea* is a different sphere of influence: it includes your own personal neighborhood, the local grocery, and people at your workplace. We are to be Christ's witnesses in those places, too. Does your faith impact the relationships you have in your *Judea*? Shouldn't Christians be the best tippers at the restaurant? The friendliest customers? The most thoughtful and diligent employees?

Take the Acts 1:8 Challenge!

Samaria was a region strictly avoided in Bible times. Samaritans were considered an inferior race of people, and were often hated and mistreated. Your *Samaria* may be people with whom you have little or no contact. How do you relate to people groups other than your own? Are you part of cliques who just ignore people who don't see things the way your group sees them? Do you go out of your way to avoid certain neighborhoods or stores or restaurants because they are owned or frequented by people whose nationality or social status makes you uncomfortable? Unlike some others of His time, Jesus never went out of His way to avoid His *Samaria*. He went straight through there and shared the Good News of His love to *all people*. Where are *the ends of the earth* for you? Maybe it's a place like India, Nicaragua or Africa, or it might be a large metropolitan area. Whatever its specific geographical locale, *the ends of the earth* is somewhere you don't usually have a connection, someplace you'd never imagine going, until God calls you to go. Every church and every one of us should ask the Lord if we are reaching out far enough in our efforts to minister to His world.

In order to ensure that we are offering God our best, most effective and well-balanced service, we must ask ourselves tough questions. Do we care more about reaching people for Christ than we do about our favorite church programs? Are we willing to find and learn new approaches to sharing Christ? Or, do we insist on hanging on to old, ineffective methods that serve our own needs and interests alone?

CHAPTER 5

MEETING REQUIREMENTS FOR EFFECTIVE CHURCH MINISTRY

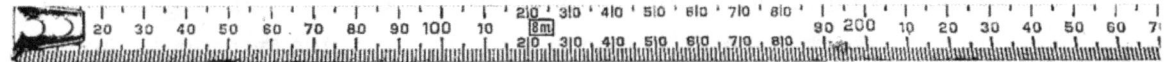

At this point in the book, you have more than likely realized again what an awesome responsibility it is to serve as a deacon. We desperately need the Spirit of God to be in charge of us and our churches. We have reminded you of some of the obstacles that churches must overcome, and you more than likely are convinced that all of us must make serious commitments to the Lord before we can serve as He desires. The Body (the church) cannot thrive when it is disconnected from the Head of the church, Jesus. Neither can our ministries within the church and in the community be successful or meaningful if we are unclear about what God requires for us to be effective. Although there are many requirements to meet before our churches can be effective, let's consider three important ones.

THE FIRST REQUIREMENT: BUILDING A STRONG FOUNDATION

You are probably familiar with the parable Jesus taught in Mt 7:24-27:

Therefore everyone who hears these words of mine and puts them into practice is like a wise man who built his house on the rock. The rain came down, the streams rose, and the winds blew and beat against that house; yet it did not fall, because it had its foundation on the rock. But everyone who hears these words of mine and does not put them into practice is like a foolish man who built his house on sand. The rain came down, the streams rose, and the winds blew and beat against that house, and it fell with a great crash.

Most of us would respond to this parable with a hearty "Amen!" Of course, we may automatically assume that our church is built on the right foundation. "Surely *we* don't need to worry about that "great crash!" Or do we?

While preparing for a deacon training event, I (Alice) decided to search the internet to determine how many churches in North Carolina were for sale. I began simply looking at churches whose brick and mortar foundations had failed, or whose buildings had literally collapsed. Then I searched for other types of collapses, such as churches whose staff or other leaders had crumpled under the weight of temptation. When I searched just for churches whose buildings were for sale, I was shocked! Scores of churches are for sale in the Atlanta and Charlotte areas, and even closer to home, in my own county. These are large churches, whose properties are worth millions of dollars! I had assumed (incorrectly) that most churches who are trying to sell their facilities are small, rural congregations whose members have aged out. But I was wrong. Even more alarming were predictions about the numbers of churches that will close their doors in the next 50 years!

What insurmountable difficulties are our churches struggling with that could make this dire prediction come true? Recently, I traveled to speak at a worship service at a church in our association. Since the service was at 11:00, I drove through town during the Sunday School hour. I was amazed at the numbers of cars I saw at local restaurants and shopping centers - evidence enough that the population of our county is sufficient to fill every church every Sunday morning. But this isn't happening. Even professing Christians do not attend church faithfully. Why? Has the church lost its effectiveness, its appeal – its heart? Why do so many people prefer to live apart from the church's influence? Do our churches *have* any influence in this day and age? Do we dare ask whether our own church could be considered successful, in any sense of the word?

What did Jesus Teach?

As leaders in our congregation, we have a desire to know how our church can have an effective ministry. The teaching of Jesus is always the best place to begin a search for answers, of course. A primary passage for understanding the church's role and the building of a successful ministry is Mt 16:13-19:

> *When Jesus came to the region of Caesarea Philippi, he asked his disciples, "Who do people say the Son of Man is?" They replied, "Some say John the Baptist; others say Elijah; and still others, Jeremiah or one of the prophets." "But what about you?" he asked. "Who do you say I am?" Simon Peter answered, "You are the Messiah, the Son of the living God." Jesus replied, "Blessed are you, Simon son of Jonah, for this was not revealed to you by flesh and blood, but by my Father in heaven. And I tell you that you are Peter, and on this rock I will build my church, and the gates of Hades will not overcome it. I will give you the keys of the*

kingdom of heaven; whatever you bind on earth will be bound in heaven, and whatever you loose on earth will be loosed in heaven."

Read closely, and you will discover five major teachings about the church:

1. What the foundation is
2. Who the corner stone is
3. How the structure is built
4. The purpose of the church
5. The authority and responsibility of the church

During a recent training event, we gave everyone a copy of the following image. The church sits atop a foundation, and at each of the four corners of the foundation, there is a building block. Participants were asked to write a word each for the foundational block and the four corner blocks that they thought best described their understanding of the foundation and building blocks of their church. With *your* church in mind, take a minute and write down your words.

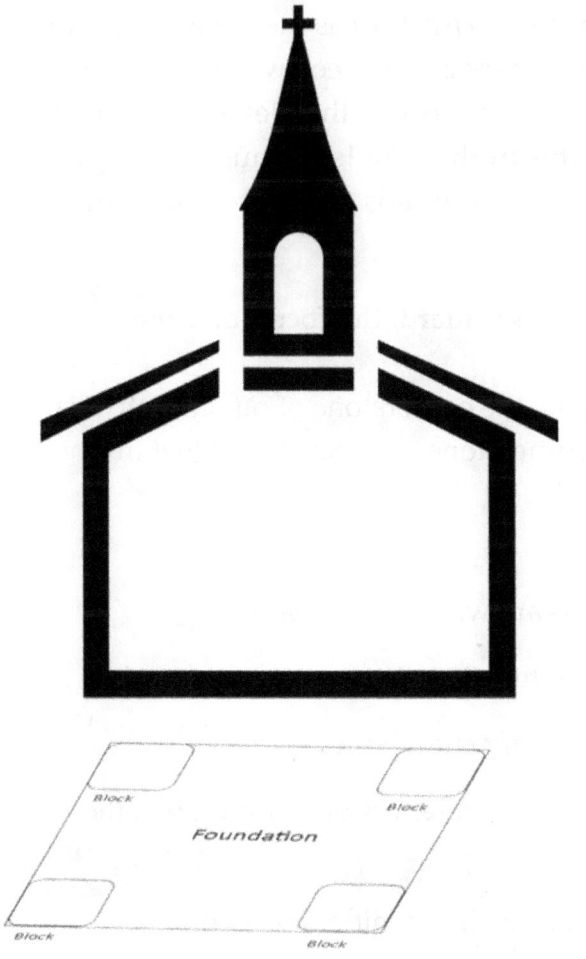

Four Corner Blocks support the building on top of the foundation.

Write a name for the foundation and each corner block.

Foundation: _____

Four Corners:

1 _____

2 _____

3 _____

4 _____

Let's compare your answers with theirs. No doubt, many of yours will be the same:

Foundation —   *Jesus Christ* was by far the predominant answer.

Corner Blocks — *Prayer* was the predominant answer, followed by *Bible study*, *Discipleship*, and *Love*.

Based on what we have been taught, these responses are what most people would probably expect. But, are these the correct answers? What did Jesus teach? Isn't it frustrating to make a solid plan, lay a good foundation, and then watch it turn into nothing?

Help From the Scriptures

Let's review Mt 16:13-19 and its five major teachings about the church:

1. WHAT THE FOUNDATION IS:

The foundation is the truth taught by the apostles and prophets and stated by Peter: "Jesus is the Messiah, the Son of the Living God."

Jesus did not say that He was building the church on *Peter*. *Petra* is the Greek word for *little rock,* which is the name Jesus gave to Simon. *Petros* is the Greek word for *big rock,* which is the truth that Peter declared when he said that Jesus is the Messiah, the Son of the Living God. Until each church realizes that this truth about Jesus must be its foundation, it will not succeed, no matter how many programs or members it boasts.

2. WHO THE CORNERSTONE IS:

The cornerstone is Jesus Himself. He must be the standard, the focus, and the purpose of all we do.

While most of us would agree that Jesus should be the cornerstone of our church, it is very difficult to determine if He is indeed that cornerstone - *in practice*, not just in principle.

Here are a few questions to consider:

    a. Do we always seek to know if our decisions are what Jesus desires?

    b. Do we always ask Him before deciding anything?

    c. Do we make decisions to please God or to pacify church members?

    d. Do we choose music styles based on our own preferences or based on whether it helps us worship and please Jesus?

    e. Do we seek to do what He did while here on earth: teaching, preaching, healing, and going about doing good?

    f. Are we obedient to our calling as a church: to win people to the Lord, to make disciples, and to build up the body of Christ until each member believes and does all that Jesus commanded us to do and to believe?

Would you say that Jesus is the Chief Cornerstone in your church?

Where is change needed?

3. HOW THE STRUCTURE IS BUILT:
Jesus' words are clear. He said, "I will build my church...."
Are we allowing Him to do the building or do we get in His way? Do we "do church" according to our own ideas, or have we asked Him? How much of what we do is simply tradition ("the way we have always done it")? Are we motivated by caution, fear, financial need, or Christ? Are there power bases in the church? (A power base is a power structure made up of families or leaders who make the decisions without input from the rest of the congregation.) It's normal to assume that we are doing God's will regarding church matters, but are we? Have we learned how to hear from Him? (See Chapter 2.) Are prayer and listening to God first priorities in our meetings? We should not assume that, when the majority of the deacons, other leaders, and the congregation agree on something, it *must* be the will of God. We must be sure that we are building the church on the right foundation!

4. THE PURPOSE OF THE CHURCH:
The purpose of the church is to storm "the gates of hell."
We must be on the *offensive*, not the defensive, if we are to be the church that does God's will. Has anyone ever described your church as "storming the gates of hell?" What image comes to mind when you hear that phrase? Is it a church that goes out into the highways and byways to find those who do not know Jesus and to bring them into the fold? Do you see your church working to reclaim those who have fallen away from Christ and His church? Can you imagine your congregation being so filled with God's Spirit that they become a people delivered from their own sins, and who free others from what imprisons them? What other pictures come to mind as you imagine your church storming the gates of hell? Can you list some reasons why your church is *not* engaging in these activities? How might you change that?

5. THE AUTHORITY AND RESPONSIBILITY OF THE CHURCH:
We have authority and responsibility because we have the keys of the kingdom.
Jesus gave His Body (the Church, *us*!) free access to the kingdom of God. It is our responsibility to help others enter through faith. We must broadcast and teach heaven's standards, God's will, and God's requirements for discipleship. But *we* have to know and do these things ourselves before we can teach anyone else!

Here are some things that we must understand before we reach out to others:

   a. Discipleship is a choice, a commitment, open to all who will accept the call.

   b. We must be empowered by the Spirit to successfully share ministry and truth with others. Teaching and ministering in our own strength will fail.

   c. Loving one another is a command, not a suggestion. It is a key way we witness to the world about their need for Jesus. Nothing impresses others so much as our love!

   d. We must bear true spiritual fruit if we want to reach the world for Jesus. The un-Christ-like behavior of Christians turns more people away from God than anything else. Hypocrisy is at the top of the list of reasons given by non-believers for not wanting to attend church. They watch our behavior. And what do they see? Too often, they see lives that do not mirror the truths we profess. They see people who act, react, and talk just like they do. When they notice that, they rightly wonder why they need God or church. Compared to believers, some non-believers are kinder, do more good works, and are better neighbors! If there is nothing different about us except for the fact that we go to church, why should they want what we claim to have? It is only when they see that our lives are different, when they see in us something good, something *unique*, that they will consider Jesus.

   e. The church's purpose is to reach out to others, and to grow in Christ-likeness.
   How well is your church doing with these two assignments? Ask yourself a few questions: How many of your church members are reaching out to the lost to win them to Jesus? How many invite people to church on a regular basis? Does your church have a regular visitation program for going out to meet people in the community who do not attend church or do not know Jesus? Would you describe most of your members as disciples of Jesus?

(Discuss these items at your deacons meetings and with your staff. If the answers trouble you, it is time to decide what can be done to *remedy the situation.*)

THE SECOND REQUIREMENT: MAINTAINING A PROPER BALANCE

The Leaning Tower of Pisa is the freestanding bell tower of the cathedral in the Italian City of Pisa. It is known worldwide, and has become a busy tourist site due to the 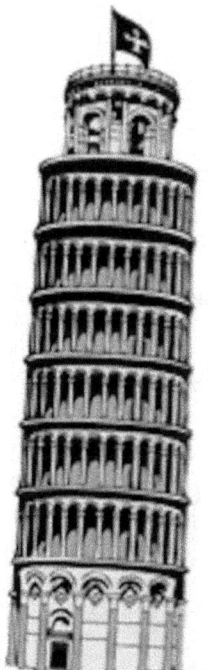 unintended tilt of the tower to one side. It is reported that the tower began to tilt during construction, caused by an inadequate foundation on ground that was too soft to properly support the bell tower. The tilt of the structure began to increase even before the structure was completed, and has gradually increased until the structure was purposefully stabilized in the late 20th century. The top of the tower is displaced horizontally 12 ft. 10 in. from where it would be if it were perfectly vertical (see *towerofpisa.org*).

Here is a thought: Could it be that our church's foundation, which is built on Jesus, is too *soft*? Could this be the chief reason we are not the church He has called us to be?

Venice is another city in Italy from which we can draw insight into the condition of our churches. The buildings of Venice are constructed on closely spaced, wooden piles, which are under water. Most of these piles are still intact after centuries of submersion. The foundations of the buildings of Venice rest on the piles, and the buildings of brick or stone sit above these footings. The piles penetrate a softer layer of sand and mud until they reach a much harder layer of compressed clay. Submerged under water with oxygen-poor conditions, wood from alder trees is used, because it does not decay as rapidly.

Alongside the strong foundation of the buildings of Venice, there is another interesting phenomenon. It has to do with the gondolas. The gondolier navigates the water canals running throughout the city. Some are wide, but some are very narrow passageways. The entire city is connected with bridges so that pedestrians can maneuver around the city. The gondolier, standing at the rear of the gondola, often has to bend down to pass safely under these bridges.

As a traveler in Venice, I (Keith) learned that the bridges are as essential to the stability of the city as the underwater piles supporting the foundations of the buildings. The bridges are what make it possible for the buildings to maintain their balance and support. Foundations are critical; balance is essential. Our churches also need balance! What does that mean? Like those interconnected buildings in Venice, no single church program or emphasis was ever intended to stand alone or be considered superior. To be balanced, a church needs *bridges* that interconnect its ministries.

How Balanced is Your Church?

Sometimes you'll hear church members and others in the community say things like:

"That's the *singing-est* church!"

"They have the most active youth program."

"If you want good preaching, go to ___ church."

"Our church has forgotten the old people."

"We're starting a visitation program. Here's a list of members to call on."

"We have to take care of ourselves before we take care of anybody else."

Have you ever wondered how people in your community describe your church? How would *you* describe your church? It might be an eye-opening exercise for your leadership to explore these questions further.

To help you evaluate the balance in your own church's ministry, complete the worksheet below. Your answers will both indicate your church's priorities and suggest areas that need your attention. Remember: balance is the key!

Place an "X" along the continuum to indicate the present emphasis in your church.

Preaching _____Music

Youth/Children _____Sr. Adult

Mission_____Maintenance

Giving _____Receiving

Rest _____Work

Love God _____Love One Another

Watch _____Pray

Trust _____Obey

Faith _____Works

Sow _____Reap

Outreach _____Care For Us

Challenge your leaders and members to share their ideas on where your church's emphasis seems to be. The results will give you an idea where to begin planning to bring your church's ministry toward the center, into balance. And don't forget that leaders need balance in their personal lives as well. When pastors, deacons, and other leaders do not lead a balanced life, the church members will be affected. *Is your personal life in balance? Why not retake the above survey, assessing the balance of your own life/ministry in these areas.* There are other categories to consider, of course, if such an assessment is to be totally accurate, but this one tool can get you started on the road to deal with any lack of balance.

Balanced Meetings

Deacons' meetings sometimes have a reputation for being boring or tedious. This is why some deacons dread them! Could it be that your meetings are out of balance? What does a typical deacons' meeting look like at your church? Before a meeting, most deacons anticipate that there will be discussions about money, conflict issues, and building maintenance. These discussions usually begin after a time of sharing community news or updates on the deacons' personal lives. In order for a meeting to be balanced, it must be adequately planned. Who plans your meetings? What is typically on the agenda? Is the agenda distributed beforehand so the deacons will be informed and prayerful? Use the following scale to assess the balance of your meetings and make any needed adjustments.

Place an "X" along each continuum to indicate the predominant emphases in your deacons' meetings:

Business _____ Prayer

Decisions _____ Faith

Action _____ Worship

Talk _____ Listening for God's voice

Feeling compassionate _____ Planning to meet needs

Jesus spoke of the need for balance. *"He who hears my words and does not put them to practice ..." (Luke 6:48).* Matthew 17:21 mentions how the disciples returned in frustration when they couldn't heal the epileptic, even though their attempt was made in the name of Jesus. Jesus told them, *"This only comes about through prayer and fasting.* James has another word for us about balance: *"faith without works is dead."* Faith is essential, but so are works. The flipside is also true: Works without faith are futile. Have you ever embarked on a course of ministry without seeking God's leadership first?

You can see how important it is to assess yourself and your church in matters of balance. If church, life, or meetings are out of balance, make a plan to change! After all, none of us wants to be described as the "Leaning Church," do we?

Another concern that church leaders should have is learning how to assess the church's effectiveness regarding its overall ministry. Churches can get off track and spend both money and time pursuing unworthy and unfulfilling goals. The next section addresses how churches can get off track and how to get them back on track.

THE THIRD REQUIREMENT: STAYING ON TRACK

One day, as I (Alice) was preparing to teach these materials on Successful Ministry, I found myself wandering down memory lane. It can be fun to revisit times you haven't thought about for many years. On that day, I recalled a childhood experience with

electric trains. My three brothers and my father all loved trains. We were one of those families whose house had an entire room devoted to the train set. In addition to several trains, we had a "town" with a train station, little houses and stores with tiny people to shop in them. I remembered the engine that smoked as its whistle blew. And there were the lights, stop signs, and switching stations, and of course, the caboose with the man standing on the rear platform. I also remembered how we kids ran the train so fast that it flew off the track, something my father didn't appreciate! Did you ever own a toy train? Have you ever ridden on a real one? Kids of all ages like trains!

Have you ever considered that in many ways churches are like trains? Churches carry people (passengers, if you will) along the track that is life's journey. Unfortunately, churches can go around in circles, just blowing smoke – or they can carry folks to real spiritual destinations. Sometimes churches run out of steam; sometimes they pick up someone who needs a lift. But they, too, can get off track. How does that happen, and how can we get them back on track when it does? This is something leaders are called to do: to evaluate the church and to do something to change any problems they find.

Let's think about trains and the train/church analogy.

First, list a few things known to cause actual train wrecks or derailments:

Here are some causes mentioned by the deacons at one of the training events:

TRAINS DERAIL BECAUSE:
1. The cars become disconnected from the engine, and travel out of control.
2. Those in charge don't know how to operate the train correctly.
3. There is a lack of cooperation between people who are running the train.
4. Obstacles, debris, or broken tracks aren't seen in time to avoid a wreck.
5. There is willful negligence on the part of the train operators.
6. The rate of speed is too fast or slow for weather or track conditions.
7. There is not enough power to run the train.
8. The operators don't know how best to reach their destination.

Do our churches get off track for some of these same reasons?
Look back over the list and circle any that might be keeping your church from making the progress it should. (You may want to discuss these in your regular deacons' meetings.)

The children of Israel often got off track in their relationship with God. Jeremiah 2 sums up their experience, and we can learn from their mistakes:

1. They strayed from God.
2. They allowed other things to take the place of their relationship with God.
3. They had leaders who did not know God or walk with God.
4. They failed to do or stop doing what God instructed.
5. They listened to the voice of a godless society, and accepted what was said as truth.
6. They lost their awe of God, and did what they wanted to do instead.
7. They abandoned God, the Spring of Living Water and dug their own broken cisterns that could not hold water. (They devised their own spirituality.)
8. They refused to acknowledge their own sin and guilt before God.
9. They refused to respond to God's conviction, choosing to go their own way.
10. They failed to ask the question: "Where is the Lord?"

Read the list again, this time circling the ones that currently describe your church.
What may have caused these problems?

What might your church leaders do to correct them? (This is another good topic for discussion in your regular deacons' meetings.)

How the Seven Churches Got Off Track [9]

Jesus spoke specifically to His churches, pointing out both weaknesses and strengths. *The following list sums up where they fell short* of His expectations. Do you think He still assesses churches today, including yours?

1. They lost their devotion for God.
2. They allowed false teaching, and engaged in worldly activities and pleasures, including sexual immorality.
3. They allowed unspiritual leaders to remain in their positions, influencing others.
4. They were unwilling to repent when God pointed out their sin.
5. They allowed spiritual apathy and deadness to remain unchallenged.
6. They failed to do what God required, even though they knew what He expected.
7. They were powerless in fighting secular influences, and failed to go through doors that God opened for them.
8. They were not aware of their own weaknesses and failures.
9. They felt adequate in themselves, not realizing that in God's eyes they were "wretched, pitiful, poor, blind, and naked."
10. They did not have repentant hearts.

Do you see any similarities to your church? Be sure to talk with your fellow deacons to find a remedy for any areas of weakness that you discover.

Principles for Staying on Track

Here are some truths to keep in mind as you prepare to move from evaluating your church to developing a plan to help your church return to the center of God's will.

1. Churches can and do get off track. A church off of its track is a serious matter.
2. Churches can keep going even when some of the "cars" are off track. Disaster will follow unless the cars are put back on track.
3. Sometimes leaders fail to consider the possibility of disaster when small derailments occur, because the church is not *completely* off track. This is a mistake.
4. It may be difficult to see just *how or where* a church has gotten off track.
5. It takes time, effort, prayer, planning, and determination to keep a church on track. It takes even more once a church has derailed.
6. God knows how best to get our church back on track, so we should ask Him.
7. Leaders are responsible to God for helping the church stay on track.
8. A church can be on track, but traveling in the wrong direction or at the wrong speed.
9. Leaders must be clear about what "being on track" looks like.
10. Prevention is always better than cure.

---

[9] Chapter 5 provides a detailed look at Jesus' analysis of the seven churches, along with the advice He gave them.

Questions to Ask

In the company of your fellow church leaders, ask these questions and discuss your ideas.

1. What are the characteristics of a church that is "on track"? Where is our church on and off track, as far as God's purpose for us is concerned?

2. How can we correct our failures? How can we prevent future failures?

3. Are we going in the right direction at the speed God desires?

4. If Jesus were given free rein in our church, what would that look like?

5. What, specifically, can we do to get our church, people, and programs back on track?

Getting Your Church Back on Track

Have you ever seen an actual train wreck? Most of us have seen one in a movie, or maybe even watched one on a YouTube video. One video that I (Keith) watched began with the train's engineer. When it was time for the train to move, he got off of the train and manually switched the track, making sure things were working as they should. The train moved along the track for a distance, until some of the cars begin to derail. At this point, it was impossible to stop the train quickly enough to prevent a domino effect, and all of the cars were affected. Whatever caused the wreck, whether it was something as big as another train in the way or something as small as a bent rail, this derailment was still a three million dollar ($3,000,000.00) disaster! Afterwards, people tried to determine the cause in order to prevent a reoccurrence.

The Hard Part

Significant life changes, such as facing health issues, starting a new job, or changing marital status, are usually accompanied by some personal soul searching. Whether such a change was planned or came unexpectedly, the person experiencing it probably laid awake at times or found him/herself lost in thought about how such a change would affect the future. A deacon may have similar experiences when evaluating his or her church, especially if there seems to have been a train wreck!

When your church has been derailed, both the leadership and the members must take time for some intense soul-searching. Difficult questions must be asked and answered. "Where are we? What is the best direction for the future?" When some are unwilling to enter into such frank conversations with one another, the situation becomes more difficult. When long-standing traditions of the church, certain influential members, and opinionated leaders are thrown together in a crisis, agreeing on and accepting change may become nearly impossible.

It isn't always the church members who resist change, however. Sometimes it is the pastor or other staff members who refuse to move forward. Our task as leaders is to create an atmosphere of open communication where everyone feels free to share what he/she believes God is saying to the church. And the church must pray to be willing to follow wherever God leads.

Here are some suggestions to help you determine how best to keep your church on track, walking in the right direction, at the right pace, as you do God's will:

1. Be willing to take an honest look at where your church might be off track, even in small areas, in programs and methods.

2. Realize that you cannot get back on track by yourselves – you need God's help. This is taught clearly in John 15. Jesus said, *"I am the vine, you are the branches. He who abides in me, and I in him, bears much fruit; for without me you can do nothing."*

3. Try to determine who is *working the switches* in your church. Who is really calling the shots? What obstacles are keeping the church from moving safely down God's track?

4. Realize that it takes time to stop the train. Forward momentum keeps it moving, even when there are cars flying off the track. This is also true of our churches. Change takes time and effort. As hard as it might be to face, there may be areas or programs in your church (or in your own life) that need to be declared a train wreck. Consider the possibility, and take any needed action. Get advice; get training for your leaders so you can implement change. Keep everyone informed, making sure the church members are involved in decision-making. Pretending the train wreck didn't really happen is *not* a good plan! Accept the fact that your church will never change direction until derailed ministries come to a halt, and a new direction is determined and implemented. When cars are derailing, the domino effect will take its toll until the train stops. This is the very danger that many churches find themselves in today, and that may lead to the closing of their doors. Ineffective ministry rarely bears healthy fruit!

5. Understand that sometimes the train's *caboose* must be cut off. A caboose was attached to the rear of the train for reasons that don't exist today:

(a) the conductor had an office in the caboose where he did necessary paper work; and (b) from the caboose, the conductor signaled the engineer with a lantern if there was a problem anywhere between the middle half of the train and the last car. Trains no longer need a caboose for these reasons.

Getting your church back on track may mean getting rid of unnecessary weight such as ineffective programs. In days past, every church (large or small, wealthy or poor, one pastor or large staff) was expected to offer the same programs if they wanted to be effective. Such expectations often led churches to stretch their staff and lay volunteers to the limits of their time and energy, resulting in a tired church membership. It is hard for a church to realize that it should only be doing what it can do with the available personnel and resources. Comparison with other churches often drives members into discouragement and burnout. For example, why would a congregation hire a youth minister for 20 youth while neglecting 100 senior adults!

6. Realize that when the *engine* is off the track, there will be no movement! Church leadership is critical to the success of the church in following its mission. The rest of the train is powerless without its engine. Leaders cannot lead without power. A leader's power does not come from a church's traditions, or from secular skills, educational degrees, or good business sense, or even from the power vested in us by the church! Our power for effective ministry comes from God and God alone. We must remember that Jesus said, "Without me you can do *nothing*!" Without His power driving our ministries, our church will veer off track with tragic consequences: we will fail to do God's will.

CHAPTER 7

FOLLOWING JESUS, THE HEAD OF THE CHURCH

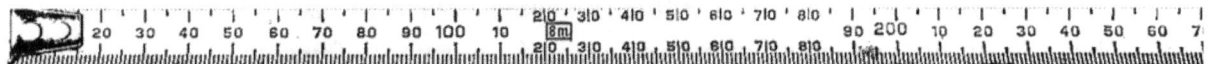

Most Christian leaders understand the doctrinal teaching that Jesus is head of His Body, the church. But, if asked what that truth means for their local congregation, leaders and members may be confused. We realize that Jesus is the Lord of everything, of course, and churches should follow His leading in all that they undertake in kingdom work. But understanding the specific responsibility in our relationship to the Head is critical. And learning to discern whether we are connected or disconnected to Jesus is imperative, if we are to be obedient in this calling.

What did Jesus say about the topic? Most of us are familiar with the conversation He had with Peter regarding the church that is found in Mt 16:15-19:

> *"But what about you?" he asked. "Who do you say I am?" Simon Peter answered, "You are the Messiah, the Son of the living God." Jesus replied, "Blessed are you, Simon son of Jonah, for this was not revealed to you by flesh and blood, but by my Father in heaven. And I tell you that you are Peter, and on this rock I will build my church, and the gates of Hades will not overcome it. I will give you the keys of the kingdom of heaven; whatever you bind on earth will be bound in heaven, and whatever you loose on earth will be loosed in heaven."*

The Bible is clear in its teachings that Jesus *is* the Head of the Church. He is its foundation as well as its cornerstone. We are His body, and as such are expected to be about His mission.

The church is to be engaged in two major activities:

1. **Doing the same kind of ministry Jesus was anointed and commissioned to do.**
   *The Spirit of the Sovereign LORD is on me, because the LORD has anointed me to **proclaim good news to the poor**. He has sent me to **bind up the brokenhearted**, to proclaim freedom for the captives and release from darkness for the prisoners, to proclaim the year of the LORD's favor and the day of vengeance of our God, to **comfort all who mourn**, and **provide for those who grieve in Zion**—to **bestow on them a crown of beauty instead of ashes, the oil of joy instead of mourning, and a garment of praise instead of a spirit of despair*** (Is 61:1-3).

2. **Helping fellow members to be edified** (through utilizing their spiritual gifts) **and engaged in ministry** to each other and to the community. (Some of this means helping members settle disputes – see Mt 18:15-17.)

Take a few moments to think about how well your church is doing in these two areas.

JESUS, THE HEAD OF THE CHURCH, ACCORDING TO PAUL

In his letters to the churches, Paul often spoke of his concern for them, and wrote with the express purpose of helping them overcome problems that they encountered. He felt he was commissioned by God to be a servant of the churches (Col. 1:25). Some of the many topics he addressed were: helping them to know how to structure the church, how to use their gifts to minister to others, the importance of reaching out to others, and what qualifications its leaders should have. He also expressed concern that churches be faithful in helping other Christians who were struggling. In his comments about Jesus being the Head of the church, he mentioned some of the following truths:

1. God appointed Jesus to be head over everything for the church, which is his body, the fullness of Him who fills everything in every way (Eph 1:22-23).

2. He said that God's purpose for establishing the church was that *through the church the manifold wisdom of God should be made known to the rulers and authorities in the heavenly realms* (Eph 3:10).

3. He wrote that glory should be brought to God via the church (Eph 3:20-21).

4. He says that Jesus is the head of the church, His body, of which He is Savior (Eph 5:26).

5. He reminded readers that Christ loved the church, giving Himself up for her to make her holy, cleansing her by the washing with water through the word (Eph 5:27-28).

6. He taught that Jesus, who is the beginning, the firstborn from the dead, is the head of His body, the church, and in all things He must be preeminent (Col 1:18).

It is important for us as leaders to examine our own lives as well as helping our church consider its relationship to Jesus, Head of the Body. Use the questions that follow for this purpose.

AM I ALLOWING JESUS TO BE THE HEAD (LORD) OF MY LIFE?

1. Do I tend to make decisions without consulting Jesus?
2. Do I always spend time in prayer before making an important decision?
3. Is it easy for me to step out in faith when I do not know the specifics of how things will turn out?
4. Have I seen God do something in my life recently that can only be explained as being a God-thing?
5. Am I as excited about the Lord and committed to His ministry as I have ever been?
6. Am I the kind of leader whom people respect and want to follow?
7. If I allowed Jesus to be Lord of my life in every area, what changes would have to be made? What would I have to start or stop doing?
8. Am I consistent in my commitment to the Lord and His church?

QUESTIONS FOR YOUR DEACON BODY TO CONSIDER AND DISCUSS:

1. Why is it so important for the body of Christ to be connected to its head?
2. What does a connected church look like?
3. What does a disconnected church look like?
4. What can we, as leaders, do to help our churches be vitally connected to Jesus?
5. Who is the most influential person or family in your church?
6. How are decisions made, budgets decided, leaders elected, etc.?
7. How much time do you and the other leaders spend in prayer before making a decision about something in the church? Do you ask the members to join you in prayer about the decision(s)? How major a decision does it have to be before you ask for prayer?
8. Other than a building project, when was the last time your church took a leap of faith in some area?
9. When was the last time something happened in your church that could only be explained as God at work?
10. How easy is it for your church to make changes?

11. Are there ministries/programs/leaders in your church that are no longer effective?
12. What would your church look like if Jesus were allowed to function as the Head of your church? Would anything change?

CONNECTED OR DISCONNECTED?

One of the most difficult tasks of leaders is to be objective when assessing the strengths and weaknesses of the congregation. Because we love the church and want the best for it, sometimes we fail to see its strengths and are blind to its weaknesses. Sometimes we are overly critical, and at others times we are defensive. But until we are willing to ask God to show us the strengths and weaknesses as He sees them, we will probably not make much progress.

All of us want to believe that our church is allowing Jesus to be its Head. But is it? Coming to a better understanding of what a church looks like that is connected to Jesus will be helpful in our self-evaluation. We most certainly do NOT want to be like a decapitated chicken, running around as if it is still alive, when in reality it is dead!

Characteristics of a Connected Church

If our church is vitally connected to Jesus, its rightful Head, what does that look like? Although the following characteristics are not all-inclusive, they are a good place to begin your evaluation.

1. *The church will be unified.*
In His priestly prayer, recorded in John 17, Jesus prayed that His church be unified. Thankfully, He included a definition of unity: *that we would be one as He is with the Father and as the Father is with the Spirit.* The Godhead does not have a moderator to ensure their unity. They are of one heart and one mission. And Jesus prayed that the body of Christ would grow into that same oneness. Unfortunately, our *oneness* is often voided by personal preference, selfishness, and lack of spiritual maturity. But there is still hope! There is hope when the body of Christ makes a commitment to allow Jesus to be Lord of everything.

2. *The church will be generous.*
We cannot examine the life and ministry of Jesus without being aware of His many acts of giving. He gave to those in need of healing, encouragement, love, direction, and His final act of giving was His own life for our salvation. And His servant Paul wrote much about how we should give to others in need, meeting the needs of the universal church wherever it is gathered.

Sometimes we measure our giving simply by dollars or a percentage of our budget. And financial giving is an important part of the mission of the church in the world. But Jesus expects us to give of ourselves, (our time and our talents and our spiritual gifts), to help build up the body and to reach the world. Generosity on all levels will be the mark of a connected church.

3. *The church will want to reach out to others.*
Jesus came to earth with a mission from the Father. He came to earth to seek and to save those who were lost, and to make disciples of those who would believe in Him. When a church is connected to Jesus, it will have a clear understanding of His mission, and that He has called them to carry out His purposes. It is so easy to turn our eyes and hearts inward and never see the needs of those outside the doors of our church. It is too easy to relegate the fulfillment of Christ's mission to the pastor and missionaries.

The church with a heart for those inside the church walls, as well as compassion for those in the community and the world, is a church where Jesus is the Head. We must ask Him to help us see the multitudes that are wandering through life without Him. How is your church doing with this focus on mission?

4. *The church will be dependent on the Father.*
Unfortunately, we can be fooled into thinking we are dependent on God, when we are really depending on certain members, our staff, and our ability to pay our own way. We seem to call on God in earnestness only when emergencies arise!

I (Keith) have had the privilege of going on mission trips to Nicaragua several times in the last ten years. Every time I go, I am overwhelmed by the spirit of the people there. They are hardworking and generous, even though they have very few resources. They completely depend on God's provision for their daily bread.

Jesus taught that we can do nothing without Him. Have you considered that this was one way of reminding us that we cannot do His will on our own? In America, we are extremely blessed. We are so blessed that we no longer know what it means to "pray for our daily bread." Because of our affluence, we can easily forget to be thankful for many blessings. The key to unlocking true blessings from God is directly connected with our dependence on Him. When we minister in His power and strength, He will work in ways that we cannot imagine. The church where Jesus is Head is aware of this truth, and experiences the wonder that comes from dependence on Him. It has discovered that dependence is a position of strength and not weakness.

5. *The church will be connected to other churches.*
A church that has Jesus as its Head will realize and celebrate the truth that we are one body, with many members, that reaches across the globe as well as down the street. Churches in South America or China are part of us, and we are part of their ministry. When churches join together as one to minister in Jesus' name, it brings joy to the heart of God. He delights in churches that join hearts together through prayer and shared dependence on Him!

    No single congregation or denomination can reach everyone in the world for Christ. No single church can meet the needs of hurting people or bring every lost person to Christ. Every church must serve alongside each other to fulfill the Great Commission of our Lord. Competition will never be a factor when Jesus is the head of the church. Unfortunately, too many churches and church staff choose to isolate themselves, choosing not to connect with other churches in ministry and mission.

    When churches are connected to Jesus as Head, there will be an awareness and kinship with believers all over the world, as well as intense prayer for the persecution that many of our brothers and sisters in Christ face daily. Some alarming statistical information about suffering and persecution is available on the internet, including the fact that 322 Christians are martyred for their faith and 214 churches are destroyed ... each month! [10]

    Persecution connected the early church, and persecution can be a connecting point for believers today. The Church that has Jesus as Head will face the assaults of Satan and great persecution. It we are free from this type of persecution, we can be grateful. But it is our responsibility to our fellow Christians to be in prayer for them. One day, it will happen even in America. The same Jesus will sustain us through persecution, and embolden us to keep the faith.

    There seemed to be little confusion in the minds of the early disciples as to Who should be Lord of the universal church as well as Head of each local congregation. And the commission that Jesus gave to His followers just prior to His ascension into heaven is surely the heart of the church's mission today. When a church is vitally connected to the Head, it will be doing what Jesus commanded it to do.

---

[10] https://www.opendoorsusa.org/christian-persecution/

Being a Great Commission Church

One of the most familiar, but perhaps least understood, passages of the New Testament is called the *Great Commission*. Song after song has been sung about it; every mission group has studied it. And there's probably not a preacher who hasn't preached on the *commission* that Jesus gave to His disciples before He returned to the Father. We have all heard it, but do we remember it well?

Complete the following quiz: WHAT DO YOU REMEMBER?

True or False?
1. _____ The Great Commission was given to the disciples before Jesus' death and resurrection.
2. _____ The Great Commission was given only to the first disciples that Jesus called to follow Him.
3. _____ By the time the Great Commission was given, those who heard it were convinced Jesus had been raised from the dead, and were committed to following Him.
4. _____ The Great Commission was given to the disciples when they were assembled in Jerusalem.
5. _____ The Great Commission was given 40 days after Jesus' resurrection.

Short Answer:

6. What did Jesus say about Himself before He commissioned the disciples?

7. How did Jesus encourage them to keep His commission?

8. The Great Commission includes 3 things Jesus expects of His disciples. What are they?

Check your answers: (Refer to Mt 28:16-20.)

True/False:

1. <u>False.</u> Although Jesus sent them out on some mission trips, the Great Commission was not given until just before His ascension into heaven.

2. <u>True and False.</u> Technically speaking, only the eleven were present when the Great Commission was first given; however, every believer is under the same orders to share the gospel to the ends of the earth.

3. <u>False.</u> Note, in verse 17, the sobering words "but some doubted." Even though the disciples had spent three years with Jesus, some still struggled with disbelief.

4. <u>False.</u> Jesus directed the disciples to meet Him on the mountain in Galilee.

5. <u>True.</u> Acts 1:3-11 tells us that Jesus appeared to believers over a 40-day period after his resurrection from the dead. Then He ascended into heaven. The commission was given at the site of the ascension.

Short Answer:

6. *What did Jesus say about Himself before He commissioned the disciples?*
   Jesus reminded them that all authority on heaven and earth had been given to Him. Because of His authority He could give this assignment and expect obedience.

7. *How did Jesus encourage them to keep His commission?*
   He reminded them of His continuing presence with them always.

8. *The Great Commission includes 3 things Jesus expects of His disciples. What are they?*
   a. To go (or, as they were going) and make disciples of all nations.
   b. To baptize converts in the name of the Father, the Son, and the Holy Spirit.
   c. To teach new believers to obey everything He commanded.

How well did you remember the Great Commission? Did you discover anything new about it … or about yourself?

Athletic programs have long been popular with churches. These programs are great avenues for reaching out to the unchurched. The deacons of one church met to develop guidelines for a church softball team, specifically centering on rules for prospective players. They discussed several questions. How many Sundays will a player have to attend worship? Will they be required to attend Sunday School and Wednesday night Prayer Meeting?

After some lengthy discussion, they asked for the pastor's input. He obliged, saying, "If you take what you've just discussed to the church, and it passes, then we would be requiring more of our softball players than we do of our deacons!" As you can imagine, those present became very quiet. We do tend to require more from others than we expect of ourselves at times, don't we? But Christ expects obedience from *all* of us. How well do you keep His commands? What about your church? Are you working diligently on this all-important assignment from Jesus?

Perhaps one of the most overlooked portions of the Great Commission comes at the end: to teach people to obey everything that Jesus commanded. *That* is a tall order, to be sure! The following survey is taken from a compilation of studies done by various individuals who posted them on the internet. Take a few moments and thoughtfully examine yourself regarding the following commands of Jesus.

How Well Are You Keeping Jesus' Commands?

Rate yourself as objectively as possible.

The Command:

	Low		Average		Good
1. Be perfect because your Father in heaven is perfect.	1	2	3	4	5
2. Pray for the Lord to send out laborers into the harvest.	1	2	3	4	5
3. Abide in me and bear much fruit.	1	2	3	4	5
4. Keep my commandments.	1	2	3	4	5
5. Love God with all your heart, soul, mind, and strength.	1	2	3	4	5
6. Love your neighbor as you love yourself.	1	2	3	4	5
7. Deny yourself, take up your cross, and follow me daily.	1	2	3	4	5
8. Pray for and love your enemies.	1	2	3	4	5
9. Don't judge others.	1	2	3	4	5
10. Let the light of your good deeds shine in order to honor me.	1	2	3	4	5
11. Reconcile with any offended brother.	1	2	3	4	5
12. Don't be a religious show-off.	1	2	3	4	5
13. Lay up treasures in heaven, not on earth.	1	2	3	4	5
14. Don't worry about tomorrow. Seek God's kingdom.	1	2	3	4	5
15. Be a person of prayer, not a vain babbler.	1	2	3	4	5
16. Practice the golden rule (treat others as you want them to treat you).	1	2	3	4	5
17. Watch for the Lord's return and be ready.	1	2	3	4	5
18. Forgive others; don't hold grudges.	1	2	3	4	5
19. Observe the Lord's Supper sincerely to remember me.	1	2	3	4	5
20. Search the Scriptures to learn about me.	1	2	3	4	5

Evaluation:

Add all the numbers you have circled and check below:

_____
(your score)

71-100 Above Average
50-70 Average
20-49 Below average. Get to work!

The best way to use this information is to look at the commands where you are *not* doing well, and work on them. Deacons can also use this tool to evaluate their churches. When weaknesses are identified, you should pray and make a plan to encourage your church's increasing obedience to Jesus' commands. (The information that follows is useful for such planning.)

A Portrait of Great Commission Deacons and Churches

Most of us agree that the need to fulfill the Great Commission is an urgent one, but sometimes we are at a loss to know how. If you want to be a Great Commission Deacon, and you want your church to be a Great Commission Church—let this be the beginning of your quest!

Perhaps one of the greatest reasons that we are not doing well obeying the Great Commission is that we have failed to keep the *Great Commandment*:

> *...while he was eating with them, he gave them this **command**: "Do not leave Jerusalem, but wait for the gift my Father promised, which you have heard me speak about. For John baptized with water, but in a few days you will be baptized with the Holy Spirit* (Acts: 1:4).

We must **BE** *(empowered by the Spirit)* before we **DO** *(attempt to serve)*. Never forget that working in the strength of the flesh instead of the power of the Spirit always leads to failure. Two examples in the Scripture will help us understand this important truth:

1. BEFORE Peter was filled with the Spirit, he was prideful, impetuous and cowardly. AFTER his empowerment, he was bold, preached powerful messages, wrote encouraging and instructive letters, and became a powerful vessel of truth.

2. BEFORE Paul was filled with the Spirit, his natural zeal and religious enthusiasm led him to kill. AFTER his empowerment, he became a missionary for Jesus and perhaps the greatest Christian in history.

A Glimpse of the First Great Commission Deacons

It is helpful to examine the traits of the first deacons, as recorded in Acts 6.

1. They exhibited spiritual character, and had a good reputation. They were known as those who walked daily with God, and were obedient to His Spirit.

2. They were full of God's Spirit: Spiritual fruit was evident in their lives.

3. They were full of God-given wisdom.

4. They were willing to take up the responsibility of service in order to free the ministers to pray and to minister the word.

5. They were full of faith.

6. They were full of God's grace and power.

Self-Evaluation

Answer these questions:

How would you rate yourself on these traits?

What can you do to improve in any of these areas?

Would it make a difference if the deacons on your board had these traits? How?

When Deacons Follow the Great Commission...

Wouldn't it be wonderful if church leaders followed the Great Commission? Have you wondered what difference it could really make?

Consider what happened when the first deacons chose obedience:

1. The word of God spread.
2. The numbers of disciples increased rapidly.
3. A large number of priests became obedient to the faith.
4. They were able to do great wonders.
5. They were able to withstand opposition.
6. They were able to preach and teach the Scriptures.
7. They were able to forgive those who attacked them.
8. They were sensitive to the Spirit's leadership.
9. They overcame their prejudices and witnessed to different races and nationalities.

Answer these questions:

Do you think this behavior and its results are even possible in today's world? Why or why not?

How does your life measure up to this snapshot of the first deacons?

What might you do to improve your "score"?

> In a nutshell,
> Great Commission deacons are:
>
> 1. Empowered by the Spirit.
> 2. Life-style evangelists (being God's witnesses and sharing Jesus in everyday life).
> 3. Disciple-making disciples (growing spiritually and helping others to do the same).
> 4. Teachers of truth.
> 5. Dependent upon the presence of the Lord, living obediently under His authority.

Don't be discouraged—be committed and determined! The Spirit of God will do the rest. All He requires is a dedicated, willing, yielded servant.

Making Progress in Our Obedience

When deacons *do not* obey Christ's commands (whether in their personal lives or in their leadership roles), disaster is a real possibility. At one of our deacon training events in North Carolina, I (Keith) spoke to a certain young pastor. His church was reaching people, baptizing new believers. Their reputation in the community was good. This pastor was providing excellent leadership. Disaster appeared in the form of a particular deacon who had long made it his own personal responsibility to decide when a pastor's time at the church was over. This deacon had skills, but he used them for harm instead of good! He networked behind the scenes to build support for his opinion, and then made life miserable for the pastor until that pastor resigned.

Sound familiar? It should, because – sadly – this is not uncommon! If you examine the statistics on forced terminations, you will see much widespread damage is happening in our churches. Pastors and their families are emotionally and spiritually brutalized, and congregations become disillusioned with the church, with the leadership, and even with God!

Certainly, there are times when staff changes must be made, but Great Commission deacons will handle these situations in a Christ-like manner. We must remember that our actions indicate the genuineness of our walk with God!

Jesus gave His disciples a solid framework for transforming lives: we might call it the **"Great Commission Checklist."** Go…Make Disciples…Baptize…Teach.

1. *Go* to anyone who is lost, wherever they are.
   Have you ever led anyone to Christ? Have you ever tried?
2. *Make Disciples* of all who come to Christ.
   How do you help other believers become more like Christ? What does your church do to help in this important task?
3. *Baptize* those who have come to Christ.
   Baptism is an act of obedience out of gratitude for what Christ has done for us.
4. *Teach* believers "all" things that Christ has commanded us. That which we *fail* to teach eventually takes its toll.

Do you and your church follow Jesus' checklist with due diligence?
If you see areas that are lacking, do something about it!

Living As Children of the King

It is easy to become so focused on DOING what God wants us to do that we forget the joy and privilege of simply BEING His child. Jesus wants us to find joy in our relationship with Him as well as in our service for Him.

This survey will guide you in a time of self-examination.

<u>Doing Great–Doing OK–Need Help</u>

1. It is easy for me to understand what God wants me to do.	1	2	3	4	5
2. I am daily living the kind of lifestyle that is pleasing to God.	1	2	3	4	5
3. It is easy for me to focus on God rather than on myself.	1	2	3	4	5
4. I could describe my life as "being on fire for God."	1	2	3	4	5
5. I forgive people who hurt me, and do not hold grudges.	1	2	3	4	5
6. I am more concerned with what God wants than what I want.	1	2	3	4	5
7. I am growing in my spiritual life and see evidence to prove it.	1	2	3	4	5
8. I believe God would describe my life as being "on His path."	1	2	3	4	5
9. I am just as concerned about helping others in need as I am about meeting my own needs.	1	2	3	4	5
10. I am very concerned about doing what is right, even when it means personal sacrifice for me.	1	2	3	4	5
11. I can stand up for what is right, even when others try to persuade me to do otherwise.	1	2	3	4	5
12. I am deeply concerned that people are not ready for heaven, and I am actively trying to reach them with the gospel.	1	2	3	4	5
13. My life could be described as peaceful and joyful.	1	2	3	4	5
14. I am living a righteous life, willing to do what God wants.	1	2	3	4	5
15. I am filled with God's Spirit, and I live a powerful life.	1	2	3	4	5
16. I am determined to be obedient to the Lord, and to follow wherever He leads.	1	2	3	4	5

Evaluation:
How are you doing?
Where do you need to improve?
What commitment will you make?

THE HEART OF THE MATTER: RECOVER THE AWE

How can we help our church grow?
I just feel like something is wrong at our church.
I wonder why we don't feel the Lord's presence in our church like we used to?
Why don't we have visitors anymore?

Have you ever heard – or asked – these questions? Do you know what typically happens in a church when these questions begin to surface? When people try to answer those questions, unfortunately sometimes the 'blame games' begin: *this is someone's fault (certainly not mine!), and that someone should pay!* Sadly, pastors and other leaders make especially handy scapegoats. Deacons who find themselves embroiled in these controversies feel helpless and become frustrated. When the pressures of conflict build and the casual comment that 'something has to be done' becomes a battle cry, leaders can find themselves making hurtful decisions.

It may be that we are not asking the right questions. If we ask the wrong questions, we will not find helpful answers. We may not be thinking comprehensively when things start going downhill at church. It may be that we shouldn't be asking "What's wrong here?" and "Who is to blame?" The question we should be posing is "What is the heart of the matter?" So, when questions like those listed above begin cropping up in your church, ask yourself just what *is* the heart of the matter. Could the answer possibly be that we need to recover the awe?

Awe, as defined in Webster's dictionary, is "an emotion that combines honor and fear and respect." It is "reverential fear, the emotion inspired by contemplation of the sublime."

Awe, as defined in the Bible, is the reaction we experience when we encounter God as Majestic in Holiness, Awesome in Glory, and Working Wonders (Ex 15:11).

Awe is the natural reaction of sinful humans to a Holy God. When we encounter the majesty and power of Almighty God, we are stricken by our own sinfulness and inadequacy. God is infinite; we are finite. God is strong; we are weak. Remember the experience of Isaiah the prophet when he encountered Holy God in the Temple?

> *In the year that King Uzziah died, I saw the Lord, high and exalted, seated on a throne; and the train of his robe filled the temple. Above him were seraphim, each with six wings: With two wings they covered their faces, with two they covered their feet, and with two they were flying. And they were calling to one another: "Holy, holy, holy is the LORD Almighty; the whole earth is full of his glory." At the sound of their voices the doorposts and thresholds shook and the temple was filled with smoke. "Woe to me!" I cried. "I am ruined! For I am a man of unclean lips, and I live among a people of unclean lips, and my eyes have seen the King, the LORD Almighty."*
>
> *Then one of the seraphim flew to me with a live coal in his hand, which he had taken with tongs from the altar. With it he touched my mouth and said, "See, this has touched your lips; your guilt is taken away and your sin atoned for."*
>
> *Then I heard the voice of the Lord saying, "Whom shall I send? And who will go for us?" And I said, "Here am I. Send me!" (Is 6).*

That must have been a truly *awesome* experience for Isaiah! He saw his own sinfulness in comparison to the holiness of God, and he was awestruck. He responded with confession and repentance. Encounters with the holiness of God always spark contrition. Could it be that sinfulness is blocking the Spirit's blessings to your church? Is there weeping over sin at your church—or in *your own* prayer closet? How often do your church members walk the aisle in church to kneel and pray before God?

Notice that Isaiah's experience of seeing the holiness of God also enabled him to hear the voice of God. Our sinfulness will prevent us from hearing God. Isaiah's experience also led him to volunteer for service. Our nominating committees would probably be pleased if God's people experienced His holiness, repented of their sins, heard His voice, and volunteered for service! Imagine—no more *begging* people to volunteer for church work!

How Did We Lose the Awe?

Before we can *recover* the *awe*, we'll probably have to do some soul-searching to discover how we lost it in the first place. What went wrong? How did we become like the Ephesian church that 'lost its first love', or the Laodicean church that became lukewarm? Are we somehow tolerating false teachers like the church at Pergamum? Are we allowing strong-willed but unspiritual people to lead us, as did the church at Thyatira? Does God see us as sleepy – or dead – like the church at Sardis?

*Consider whether any of the following have led to your congregation's loss of the **awe**:*

1. Prayerlessness. There is not a strong emphasis in the church on the need for prayer.

2. Failure to seek the mind of God before making decisions.

3. Leaning on the wisdom of some strong leaders instead of on God.

4. Allowing sin and disobedience to remain unchallenged in the church.

5. A lack of strong teaching on the cost and responsibility of discipleship.

6. Failure to identify spiritual gifts, not allowing the Spirit to use us in Kingdom service.

7. Neglecting Bible reading and serious study of the Scripture.

8. The mind-set of self-sufficiency overriding the mind-set of dependence upon God.

9. A lack of fervor to reach souls.

10. Disunity and conflict among members.

These are some (not all) of the ways we can lose the *awe*, thereby quenching and grieving the Spirit of God. Take time to thoroughly discuss this topic in a deacons' meeting. After you ask the Lord to guide your thinking, list the reasons why *your* congregation may have lost its *awe*.

While you are soul-searching and evaluating, don't forget the two main causes of the loss of *awe*: Self and Satan. Self is not in awe of God, because it is absorbed in awe of itself. When concern arises over the loss of *awe* in your church, you can be sure that your Self is looking for someone to blame – someone *else!* It's so easy to see another's faults, but so hard to admit our own.

Why? Because:
- (1) We are easily deceived;
- (2) We prefer earthly satisfaction to heavenly peace;
- (3) We have an inward and downward pull away from God.

Self (the old nature within us) constantly whispers in our ears that we deserve to be the rulers of our own lives. "*You* should have the place of honor," it whispers. "They should be *glad* to follow your lead. After all, you're smart…you know best…and you rule, right?" Until we are able to identify the lies that our own old natures whisper to us, we will never get to the heart of the matter of *recovering the awe* of God.

Satan has nothing but hatred for God and God's children; never doubt that. One of his main missions is to destroy our fellowship with God. He knows that he cannot rob us of our salvation, but do we forget that he *can* still wreak havoc in our churches? He is well aware of what God hates and what grieves the Spirit, and he would like nothing better than to get you to do those very things.

What are some of the ways he attacks the church?

1. He blinds our eyes to truth about ourselves and others, about what is important, etc.

2. He tells us to focus on anything except God.

3. He lies to convince us that particular sins or weaknesses are not that important.

4. He sows discord among believers, and urges people to hold onto hurt and grudges.

5. He convinces people that there is no real need to abandon or confess sin.

6. He convinces us that prayer is useless, and that we do not have time for Bible study.

7. He persuades us to involve the children in community activities and sports, even if they have to miss church repeatedly.

On and on go his lies, and over and over we trip and fall!

What Does God Expect?

If we are to reclaim the *awe of God*, we must meet God's expectations. Sometimes we are so busy asking God to do things for us and our churches, that we don't take time to consider what He might want from us! Consider this passage:

> *And now, Israel, what does the LORD your God ask of you but to fear the LORD your God, to walk in obedience to him, to love him, to serve the LORD your God with all your heart and with all your soul, and to observe the LORD's commands and decrees that I am giving you today for your own good? (Dt 10:12-13).*

According to this passage, God expects these things of us:
1. To be people who revere Him.
2. To be people who are willing to walk in His ways.
3. To be people who serve Him with all of our hearts.
4. To be people who obey His commands.
5. To be people who worship Him in the splendor of His holiness.

Are these behaviors obvious in your life?

What about in your church?

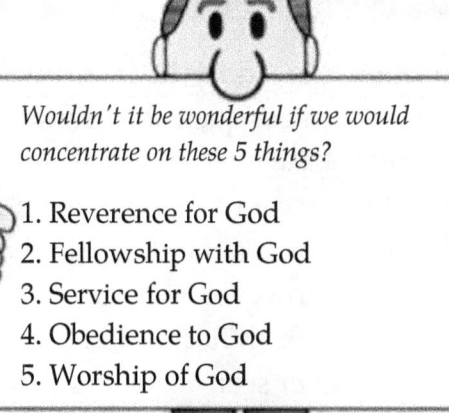

What are you going to do to *recover the awe*?

RECOVERING THE AWE

We have seen that the heart of the matter of fulfilling the Great Commission is living in *awe* of God. We have seen how many things work against that, making it easier for us to lose the *awe* than to keep it. Some of us are beginning to realize that *we* and others have lost the *awe of God,* and we want it back! We understand that it will take repentance and a commitment to meet God's expectations – by leaders and members of the congregation.

Think about the word *awesome*. It is a bit overused these days, isn't it? Anything from sneakers to sports teams to finding a deal at the flea market can be *awesome!*  To be fair, more than likely everyone thinks *something* is *awesome*. But probably not everyone thinks the same things are awesome. If it's the fastest roller coaster in the world for one, it might be Fourth of July fireworks choreographed to music on the Boston harbor for another. It depends on what you think is awesome, doesn't it? For me (Keith), it was watching Nick Wallenda walk across Niagara Falls on a tightrope, and then hearing him share his experience of the wonder of God as he made his way over the raging waters. When we do not have any other word adequate to describe our experience, we say, "That was awesome!"

True *awe* – the most awesome *awe* – is our response when we encounter God. And shouldn't we encounter God every day? Do we practice the presence of God daily? We should keep from wandering in and out of His presence. We must learn how to stay put! It seems, however, that our sense of the *awe* of God rises and falls according to our circumstances. Such fluctuations tax our spiritual vitality.

If you've ever seen a video of a shipwreck, you probably noticed the silt that collected on it while it sat on the ocean floor. The first thing that must be done when such a ship is located is to remove the silt. If this is not done, the silt will engulf the entire ship and all of its contents, preventing anyone from discovering any treasure that is there. The same is true of the Christian life. We, of course, in many ways are like a wrecked ship. If we think of the silt as sin, we can know that God is the treasure hunter who comes seeking to find what is lost. We wrecked our lives and sank to the bottom of the ocean. And even when we become Christians, we can wander out of the presence of God so often that we eventually shipwreck our lives again.

Some years ago, a pastor friend of mine moved to a church across the state. He went with great hope that God would work powerfully in that church and community. After several months, however, he became discouraged because the church seemed to have no desire to reach people for Christ. Every initiative he tried was blocked. He soon concluded that he would do the best thing possible: he would pray. He told no one, but every morning found him at the church, praying for God to move in His church members.

Some weeks went by. Some of the men, who had noticed the pastor's vehicle every day at the church early in the morning, asked him why he was at the church so early. When he told them what he was doing, they decided to join him. God began to answer their prayers and stir in the hearts of the members. More people came to the church to pray. Members began witnessing to others who gave their hearts to Christ. The church began to grow in ways no one could have imagined.

Today, that church is still strong, even though this pastor has since died. It is still a praying church. In fact, they built a prayer room with an outside entrance that is open 24 hours a day for anyone in the community to come and pray. I believe their emphasis on prayer, which began with this pastor, was used mightily by God to clean off the silt that had covered them. The removal of the silt enabled them to *recover the awe.* When God restored their *awe,* they began to share their *awesome* Savior with unbelievers, and God increased the treasure.

When we come into God's presence willing to encounter Him, when we come willing to repent and let him clear away the silt, then He can reveal His Glory. God will once again work freely in us and in our church, and we will have our *awe* back!

What the Awe of God is NOT

We need to think a bit more about this *awe,* so that we do not mistake it for mere entertainment, slick promotions and manipulation, or emotionalism. The *awe* of God is NOT a spectacle for our entertainment. There were many who followed Jesus who were amazed by His healings and miracles. Once, when the people pressed Him to perform miracles for them, Jesus rebuked them. In essence, he told them, "No more miracles." The crowds lost sight of the reason Jesus performed miracles. It was not to entertain or to gain popularity. It was to meet the needs of people. Jesus performed miracles so that people would come to believe that He was the Savior. The *awe* of God results in wonder that leads to belief. True *awe* is not found in the response, "WOW! COOL!" True *awe* is found in the response, "Now I believe!"

We cannot manufacture true *awe* out of skilled oratory, music videos, or artistic PowerPoint productions. Ann Graham Lotz shares that, on any given Sunday, "we can have video, music, drama, venues, all the cool stuff, and *still miss it* ... still miss Jesus and the awe of who He is." When did you last walk out of your church filled with the awe of God? We need to come to church each Sunday seeking the awesome presence of God, just as if we were on a treasure hunt. We need to begin every day of our lives seeking the awesome presence of God. The *awe* of God should be the foundation of every ministry. If we are going to touch lives for Christ, then our ministry – whether we are pastors, staff, deacons, or laity – must be lived out of the *awe* of God.

Ministry Flowing From the Awe of God

If anyone ever experienced the awe and wonder of God, it was Moses. From the saga of Israel's deliverance from Egypt to the receiving of the Ten Commandments on the mountain and beyond, Moses experienced the *awe*. The *awe* of God kept Moses from giving up. The *awe* of God strengthened Moses' faith and trust in God.

Eli, a priest in the Old Testament, lost his sense of the *awe*. When we lose our sense of the *awe* of God, sin slowly but surely creeps back into our lives. Eli ministered as priest, but he was not faithful: there was sin in the lives of his sons that he refused to confront. The effectiveness of his ministry as priest was diminished when disobedience crept in. But Samuel, Eli's young servant, did have a sense of the *awe* of God. How do we know that? He heard the voice of God. God spoke to him and called Samuel to serve Him. Samuel was obedient, even to the point of confronting Eli, his priest and mentor, about his sin! The *awe* of God opens our ears to His voice, and helps us to be willing to do whatever He calls us to do.

Numerous accounts in the scriptures show us the responses of men and women who experienced the *awe* of God. Two examples are Isaiah and Peter:

Isaiah responded by acknowledging that he was a man of unclean lips; then he committed himself to doing whatever God wanted him to do.

When ***Peter*** preached on the Day of Pentecost, everyone was filled with *awe*. Peter did not cause the *awe*. The *awe* came over the people because Peter preached about "This Jesus!" and they found themselves in the presence of the Holy One about whom Peter preached. Remember what happened next? Many came to salvation by faith in Jesus.

And then they asked, "What shall we do?" because *awe* ALWAYS results in action!

Are you seeking the *awe* of God on a daily basis? If you will commit yourself to doing so, God may use your commitment to change both you and your church. Is it obvious to others that you are living in the *awe* of God? Your influence and witness for Christ will grow as the *awe* of God grows in your life. The silt will be cleared away and the treasure revealed as God leads you to follow His Mission of reaching the world and edifying the body of Christ.

CHAPTER 8

KNOWING AND DOING GOD'S WILL

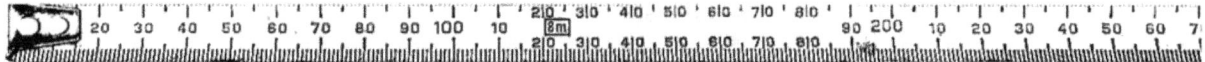

What is your church's mission? it's a question often posed to church leaders. Seminar topics and denominational publications suggest that a church can "transform its life" by following the program to be presented at a "special one-time seminar," or by purchasing and reading the latest "must-have" book. Most of us sincerely desire to be part of a church that is in the center of the will of God. The problem is that often we don't know how to discern His will. So, we jump on a bandwagon that advertises the hottest trend in Christian programming, and we are usually disappointed.

How difficult is it to discover the will of God? Is the will of God something that changes? What can we do to hear clearly from the Lord? What *is* the will of God? This is the foundational question here...and here is the short answer: *the will of God is what God wants*. Put in those terms, it is easy enough to understand. Understanding God's will becomes more complex as we seek to pinpoint the exact way(s) God wants us to serve Him. But we can be encouraged that God does indeed want us to know and to do His will. To that end, He has provided ongoing help. Our "instruction manual" is His Word, and the Holy Spirit is our guide. It is liberating to realize that God's will is knowable, and that God is eager to help us both to know and to do His will.[11] He does not hide His will from us, and His will is not hard to understand. If that is true, then why does it seem so few churches search for God's will? Why do they (the ones who *do* seek God's will) seem to have such a difficult time in knowing or doing it?

---

[11] Alice R. Cullinan, Sorting It Out: Discerning God's Call to Ministry, Valley Forge, PA: Judson Press, 1999), 29-40

WHY IT IS DIFFICULT TO DISCERN GOD'S WILL

Many reasons can explain why individuals/churches sometimes don't know God's will.

Consider these possibilities:

1. We forget to ask Him what His will is.
2. We are fearful of change, or we simply enjoy where we are.
3. We prefer tradition over change.
4. We blame others for the problem. "If they would just cooperate, we would be fine."
5. Our spiritual lives are weak. We have lost touch with God.
6. We don't know how to hear from God.
7. We are too preoccupied with problems to concern ourselves with anything else.
8. We are used to being in control and solving problems on our own.

Read the list again and mark those that you believe to be factors in your own life and church.

What can you do to make a change in your own life or in the lives of others in your church? *Write down some specific suggestions:*

PREREQUISITES FOR KNOWING THE WILL OF GOD

We believe that God wants us to know and to do His will, and we understand that God has given us the Bible (our manual) and the Holy Spirit (our guide). Isn't it reasonable to assume that, if we are having difficulty, then the problem is with us? What can we do? The Bible gives some specific guidelines.

1. We must commit the control of our lives entirely into the hands of God.

> *Therefore, I urge you, brothers and sisters, in view of God's mercy, to offer your bodies as a living sacrifice, holy and pleasing to God—this is your true and proper worship. Do not conform to the pattern of this world, but be transformed by the renewing of your mind. Then you will be able to test and approve what God's will is—his good, pleasing and perfect will (Rom 12:1-2).*

God will never make us do His will. He wants us to willingly choose to follow Him. Sometimes we cannot discern God's will because we are not committed to doing it.

2. God expects His children to be holy, to be set apart to do His will, and to live a lifestyle that is pleasing to Him.

As obedient children, do not conform to the evil desires you had when you lived in ignorance. But just as he who called you is holy, so be holy in all you do; for it is written: "Be holy, because I am holy" (1 Pet 1:14-16).

Holiness is not a topic that occupies very many minds. That alone can squash any hope we have of discerning God's will for us. He does not reveal Himself to the disobedient. So, how can we know if that is the reason for our difficulty? Ask Him!

3. Our chief goal should be to please God, and nothing pleases Him as much as doing His will. What does the "manual" say on this topic?

　a. Jesus wanted to please the Father, not Himself (Jn 5:30).
　By myself I can do nothing; I judge only as I hear, and my judgment is just, for I seek not to please myself but him who sent me.

　b. Jesus made his chief goal that of pleasing the Father (Jn 8:29).
　The one who sent me is with me; he has not left me alone, for I always do what pleases him.

　c. Paul realized the importance of pleasing God in everything (2 Cor 5:9).
　So we make it our goal to please him, whether we are at home in the body or away from it.

　d. Praying for each other is important as we seek to do the Lord's will and to please Him (Col 1:9-11).
　We continually ask God to fill you with the knowledge of his will through all the wisdom and understanding that the Spirit gives, so that you may live a life worthy of the Lord and please him in every way: bearing fruit in every good work, growing in the knowledge of God, being strengthened with all power according to his glorious might so that you may have great endurance and patience.

　e. God Himself speaks well of those who please Him (Heb 11:5 & 2 Pet 1:17).
　By faith Enoch was taken from this life, so that he did not experience death; he could not be found, because God had taken him away. For before he was taken, he was commended as one who pleased God (Heb 11:5).
　He received honor and glory from God the Father when the voice came to him from the Majestic Glory, saying, "This is my Son, whom I love; with him I am well pleased" (2 Pet 1:17).

　f. Faith is a vital part of pleasing God (Heb 11:6).
　And without faith it is impossible to please God, because anyone who comes to him must believe that he exists and that he rewards those who earnestly seek him.

g. Failure to please God leads to unanswered prayers (1 Jn 1:21-23).
Dear friends, if our hearts do not condemn us, we have confidence before God and receive from him anything we ask, because we keep his commands and do what pleases him. And this is his command: to believe in the name of his Son, Jesus Christ, and to love one another as he commanded us.

It is easy to be confused about the meaning of true commitment to God, and what doing His will entails. The allurement of the world's way of measuring success influences us more than we would like to admit. Churches even compete with each other! We should not be comparing ourselves and assessing our churches according to what other churches do. Do you remember what Jesus said when Peter seemed to be comparing himself to John?

Peter turned and saw that the disciple whom Jesus loved was following them. (This was the one who had leaned back against Jesus at the supper and had said, "Lord, who is going to betray you?") When Peter saw him, he asked, "Lord, what about him?" Jesus answered, "If I want him to remain alive until I return, what is that to you? You must follow me" (Jn 20:20-22).

TIME TO REFLECT:

1. How well is your church meeting the prerequisites for knowing God's will?

    Circle the number that best expresses where you think your church is at present. **Low Average Great**

a. Committing control of our lives entirely into the hands of God.	1 2 3 4 5
b. Displaying God's holiness by our lifestyles.	1 2 3 4 5
c. Our main focus and chief goal is pleasing God.	1 2 3 4 5
d. Much of our praying is focused on seeking to please God.	1 2 3 4 5
e. We see evidence of God's pleasure with us.	1 2 3 4 5
f. Our faith in God and willingness to do His will is strong.	1 2 3 4 5
g. We are not competing with other churches.	1 2 3 4 5

2. What can you do to strengthen your church where there is weakness?

3. What about your life? Rate your walk with God. Are you meeting the prerequisites for knowing God's will for your own life? **Low Average Great**

a. I daily commit control of my life into God's hands.	1 2 3 4 5
b. My daily lifestyle displays the holiness of God.	1 2 3 4 5
c. My main focus and chief goal is pleasing God.	1 2 3 4 5
d. Much of my praying is focused on seeking to please God.	1 2 3 4 5
e. I see evidence of God's pleasure with me.	1 2 3 4 5
f. My faith in God and willingness to do His will is strong.	1 2 3 4 5
g. I am not competing with other Christians.	1 2 3 4 5

Evaluation:
What areas of your life need to change so that you can understand God's will?

What do you need to do, or stop doing, to be faithful and obedient to God's will?

What commitments are you willing to make now to bring about those changes? Write them down.

GOD'S WILL: LESSONS FROM ADAM AND EVE

The story of Adam and Eve is a great place to start learning about God's will. It stands to reason that God's purpose for His first children is also His purpose for us. What does the Bible tell us?

1. It was the will of God that His children have fellowship with Him.
When Adam and Eve hid because of their disobedience, God called to them, "Where are you?" That same call comes to us still: "Where are you, child of God? Why do you not have time for me? Why do you not obey me? Do you not miss our sweet fellowship?" Is it possible that churches become so busy "doing church" that they fail to take time to enjoy the presence of God Himself?

2. It was God's will for the first family to experience loving relationships.
Such relationships were soon crippled. The 'blame-game' began early, and jealousy followed quickly on its heels, leading to one brother murdering the other. These tactics of the enemy are still the same, unfortunately! Do we not criticize and blame each other when things are not as we think they should be? Isn't character assassination a popular form of murder?

3. It was God's will that His children perform meaningful and productive work.
Meaningful work, however, soon degenerated into burdensome toil. This happens to us when our work is not fulfilling. How many people dread Mondays and long for Fridays? How much more tragic is it when this lack of fulfillment is found in church-related activity and work? How many people dread attending church and focus on the clock instead of worship? How many burned out leaders feel the same way?

4. It was God's will that Adam and Eve learn the lessons of obedience.
He knew that if they learned to obey, they would live fulfilled lives. His restrictions were neither grievous nor unreasonable; still, they chose not to listen. Have *you* learned that disobedience has far-reaching ramifications? After all, it is not only those who make the wrong choices who are affected by them.

How Am I Doing?
Examine yourself as objectively as possible.
Circle the number that best describes your life.

Low-Medium-High

1. I work daily on my fellowship with God:
    - a. I have a daily time of personal worship.   1 2 3 4 5
    - b. I have a daily time of prayer and Bible study.   1 2 3 4 5
    - c. I am aware of His presence throughout the day.   1 2 3 4 5
    - d. I consult Him about my daily activities and decisions.   1 2 3 4 5
    - e. I keep my sins confessed daily and specifically.   1 2 3 4 5
    - f. I forgive others readily so that my fellowship with God will not be broken.   1 2 3 4 5
    - g. I focus on listening to as well as talking with God each day.   1 2 3 4 5

2. I work daily on my relationships with family and friends:
    - a. I regularly express my love to my family and friends.   1 2 3 4 5
    - b. I do what I can to keep my relationship with family and friends strong.   1 2 3 4 5
    - c. I make quality time for family and friends.   1 2 3 4 5
    - d. I am a good listener.   1 2 3 4 5
    - e. I regularly express appreciation to friends/family.   1 2 3 4 5
    - f. People would describe me as a friendly person.   1 2 3 4 5

3. I focus on doing meaningful and productive work:
    - a. I find meaning and satisfaction in my job/retirement.   1 2 3 4 5
    - b. I believe that my work is a blessing to others, not just a way to make money.   1 2 3 4 5
    - c. I try to bear a strong Christian witness at work by what I do and say (or where you "hang out" if retired).   1 2 3 4 5
    - d. I have a "job in the Kingdom of God" and do my best to be a good steward in that role.   1 2 3 4 5
    - e. Others would describe me as a hard/faithful worker.   1 2 3 4 5
    - f. I have a good attitude at home, work, and church.   1 2 3 4 5

4. I am obedient to the Lord:
    a. I love to do whatever God wants me to do.   1   2   3   4   5
    b. I study God's Word daily to understand His will.   1   2   3   4   5
    c. I can discern when God is telling me to do
       something, or to stop doing something.   1   2   3   4   5
    d. I quickly obey when God speaks to me.   1   2   3   4   5
    e. I do not grumble and complain when God tells me   1   2   3   4   5
       to do something, or to stop doing something.
    f. I seek God's will about everything in my life.   1   2   3   4   5
    g. God would call me His obedient servant.   1   2   3   4   5

Evaluation:
Add all the numbers you have circled and check below: _____
                                                          (your score)

| 105-130 ... above average |
| 66-104 ... average |
| 25-65 ... below average |

Where do you need to be more obedient as a child of God who desires to please Him?

What will you do to make this a reality in your life?
Write out your commitment.

Were you dissatisfied with your rating on the survey? Most of us would probably say that we wish we were further along in our walk with God. Even though we may *want* to do better, we may not know where to start.

Here are some suggestions:

1. Start with your own relationship with God.
If you are not faithful in daily prayer and Bible study, begin there and keep at it.

2. Make the effort to work on your relationships...
with family members, spouse, neighbors, friends, and fellow church members. Where there are breaches, mend them.

3. Ask yourself whether your ministry (both in the church and in your personal life) is meaningful and productive.
Where there are problems, fix them. Ask for wise counsel if you are unsure what to do.

4. Be open and honest with God about any disobedience.
Confess it and correct it!

How You Can Help Your Church Obey God's Will

As individuals, we have to do our own part in being rightly related to God, and as church leaders, there are things we can do to help others.

Here are some suggestions:

1. In the area of fellowship with God:
   a. Teach, preach, and remind people that everything we do should enhance our relationship with God.

   b. Help people realize that we should not become so busy working FOR God that we forget to have fellowship WITH Him.

   c. Remind members that religious activity isn't the same as spending time with Him.

   d. Help them realize how detrimental the effects of disobedience and unconfessed sin are to an open relationship with God.

   e. Teach them what true worship is, and the necessity of worshipping during the week, as well as on Sundays.

   f. Teach them the value of prayer as both talking and listening to God.

2. In the area of loving relationships:
   a. Plan more ways for people to get to know each other on a personal basis. You might consider some of these:
      (1) Fellowships/small and large groups
      (2) Home Bible studies
      (3) Members-of-the-month info in newsletters
      (4) Pictures and write-ups about new members
      (5) Testimonies in services
      (6) Up-to-date Church Directories

   b. Emphasize families and marriages through:
      (1) Classes
      (2) Retreats
      (3) Fellowships
      (4) Conflict Management Seminars
      (5) Sermon Series

   c. Teach and preach on the need for Christians to love and to forgive each other.

   d. Develop plans/ways to minister to people in crisis.

3. In the area of meaningful and productive work in the Kingdom of God:
   a. Provide classes on spiritual gifts.

   b. Nurture an environment where everyone is expected to serve in some capacity.

   c. Allow members to volunteer to "do their passion" in some way, such as art classes for the community, building projects, etc.

   d. Plan ways to encourage and recognize those serving in various positions.

   e. Develop service opportunities for children and youth.

4. In the area of obedience:
   a. Emphasize seeking and doing God's will in all areas of life and decision-making.

   b. Teach people what to do when they have been disobedient to God.

   c. Encourage members to be forgiving and accepting of those who made mistakes and are seeking restoration.

   d. Consider accountability groups or partners to help each other learn to obey God.

Review these suggestions and *make specific plans* for helping others learn these truths. Which ones will you incorporate into your own life?

The Will of God and Your Life

Consider these statements:

- God commanded Adam and Eve NOT to do one thing – just *one* thing…
  …and they disobeyed Him.

- God gave the children of Israel ten commandments…
  …and they disobeyed every single one of them.

- Jesus summed up ten commandments into two for His disciples – just *two*…
  …and we *still* cannot keep them!

The Holy Spirit inspired the writing of the New Testament with specific instructions for us. Here are just a few:
1. Be holy for I am holy (1 Pet 1:15).
2. Be filled with the Spirit (Eph 5:18).
3. Forgive as the Lord forgave you (Col 3:13).
4. Be devoted to one another in love (Rom 12:10).
5. Love your enemies and pray for those who persecute you (Mt 5:24).
6. Do not judge, or you will be judged (Mt 7:1).
7. Ask the Lord of the harvest to send out workers into his harvest field (Lk 10:2).
8. Go into all the world and preach the gospel to all creation (Mk 16:15).
9. Do not store up for yourselves treasures on earth (Mt 6:19).
10. Be careful not to do your acts of righteousness before men (Mt 6:1).
11. Be on guard against the yeast of the Pharisees and Sadducees (Mt 16:6).
12. Be self-controlled and alert. Your enemy the devil prowls around like a roaring lion looking for someone to devour (1 Pet 5:8).

There are many more, of course, but why not take these twelve and start leading your church toward making God's will its mission *and* its passion? Their commitment should be to SEEK His will DAILY and, by His grace and power, DO His will DAILY. And *we* must make the same commitment.

Reflections

We have discussed several important things about knowing and doing God's will. Wouldn't it be wonderful if God would send telegrams or some other sign to let us know His will for each individual and church? He understands, however, that a relationship with His children is much more important than any information He could relay to us!

Many of us don't seek God's will until we are facing hardship, sensing a loss of direction, or wondering how to respond to a life-changing experience. Those are the times when we come to realize our utter need to be in the center of God's will. But whether we are in crisis, or simply curious about knowing God's will, eventually the real question will surface: *When we finally come to know the will of God – will we be willing to follow Him in full obedience, experiencing everything that He intends for us?*

I (Keith) remember seeing a drawing of a mouse, carefully studying a mousetrap which was weighed down with a tasty-looking hunk of cheese. Since the mouse was wearing a helmet, I guess it was working on a strategy to get the cheese without getting hurt! Unfortunately, we often approach new opportunities in life the same way. We move forward cautiously, protecting ourselves because we're unsure whether this step is God's will. We prefer certainty, which sometimes makes us freeze and never move at all.

While serving as a pastor, I met a young person who felt the call of God into full time vocational ministry. He was so excited and sure of God's call that he made plans to attend a Christian university. His parents cautioned, "You need to have a backup career in case this doesn't work out." Because he loved and respected his parents, he took their comments so seriously that he began to doubt God's call. He lost that sense of certainty. As time passed, the young man moved closer to the parents' will, and further away from what he believed was God's will. This is not the only time I have heard this strategy – "I'd better have something to fall back on in case God's will doesn't work out." Why do we follow after the will of God with *trepidation* rather than with *boldness*?

If fear and doubt are hindrances to knowing the will of God, so is the wrong idea that *only clergy can know the will of God*. God does speak to those He calls into ministry, but God doesn't *only* speak to clergy! Every Christian needs to seek the will of God.

When my wife and I visited San Antonio, Texas, we visited the four Spanish Missions along the San Antonio River. Upon entering one of the missions, we saw that a rope had been hung across the aisle between the front pews. On the other side of the rope, there was a white stone in the floor. The inscription read, "Beyond Rope Is Sacred

– Do Not Enter." I thought of the Holy of Holies in Israel's Temple, where only the High Priest was allowed to enter. The thick, floor-to-ceiling curtain that separated the Holy of Holies from the rest of the Temple was called the *veil*. It was this veil that was torn from top to bottom when Jesus died on the Cross, making it possible for all who accepted His sacrifice to enter into God's presence.

It is needful for us to come daily into His presence with hearts that want to know and to do the full will of God. If you earnestly seek Him, He will be found! Are you willing to seek Him daily to discover His will? Imagine how different our lives and our churches would be if we lived by this challenge!

Read the following passages and ask God to speak to your heart.

(The Message, Romans 12:1-2):
So here's what I want you to do, God helping you: Take your everyday, ordinary life—your sleeping, eating, going-to-work, and walking-around life—and place it before God as an offering. Embracing what God does for you is the best thing you can do for him. Don't become so well-adjusted to your culture that you fit into it without even thinking. Instead, fix your attention on God. You'll be changed from the inside out. Readily recognize what he wants from you, and quickly respond to it. Unlike the culture around you, always dragging you down to its level of immaturity, God brings the best out of you, develops well-formed maturity in you.

(Eph 5:17):
Don't live carelessly, unthinkingly. Make sure you understand what the Master wants.

These passages challenge us to find God's will and to obediently follow it. As Paul teaches in Romans, we must be in the process of progressing to higher levels of maturity as we follow Christ. In other words, as we learn obedience in our current walk with God, we are called to a new level of walking with Him – one that requires a deeper level of obedience. The more obedient we become, the more we are being formed into His likeness. The will of God for Adam and Eve to learn obedience is, indeed, God's will for us, too.

Think about Peter, who was often confronted with making the right decision. When Peter *did* choose correctly, his commitment to obedience led him into a deeper relationship with God, and into a better understanding of God's will. So it can be with us. Whether we progress in our relationship with God often depends on whether we are obedient. With all of his heart, Peter wanted to follow Jesus. Even so, he sometimes fell short. Every time he obeyed God, he became stronger. As he gained strength, he was encouraged to strive for even more obedience.

What about you?
Are you growing in your obedience to God?

Answer the following questions thoughtfully.
Make whatever commitment you are *willing* to make.

1. Are you daily walking with Him?
   Do you consider yourself His faithful disciple?
   Do you know for sure that you are His child?

2. How faithful are you in reading and studying your Bible?

3. Do you consider yourself a person of prayer, one who experiences God's presence?

4. Do you faithfully worship Him…and not just in corporate worship at church?

5. Have you discovered where God wants you to serve? Are you doing so faithfully?

6. Are you a faithful steward with your tithes, time, and energy?

7. Do you faithfully pray for and witness to unsaved people God brings your way?

Sometimes we seek the will of God only in the larger issues of life, overlooking His will for our daily lives. Do your answers to the questions above place you on this side of "the rope," or do they indicate your free access into the presence of God? Disobedience or negligence in our relationship with God will put us out of fellowship with Him. With free access, you can approach the throne of God with boldness, and ask Him to show you His will for your life. Don't rely on "a backup plan," but be determined to follow Him faithfully, knowing that He will supply all of your needs. You will be blessed, and you will be a blessing! The more you are obedient to Christ, the more effective you will be as a leader in your church.

Section Three:

Handling the Administrative Tasks

9. LEARNING HANDS-ON MINISTRY STRATEGIES 169

10. MANAGING ORGANIZATIONAL TASKS 183

11. HANDLING CHURCH CONFLICT 197

LEARNING HANDS-ON MINISTRY STRATEGIES

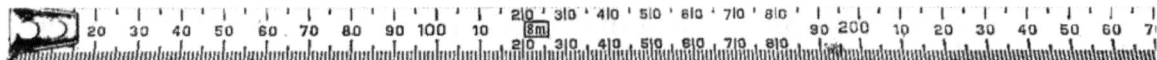

You have been called by God, and now you are serving as a deacon in your church. And you have probably learned that being called and ordained/installed does *not* equal ministry experience! Since we do not automatically know how to minister, being expected to minister in any given situation is often stressful. The good news is that there are some basic skills (easily learned) that will help you minister effectively whenever a need arises.

It is important to discover your spiritual gifts as well as your natural talents and abilities, because you need to serve out of your strengths, not your weaknesses. It is encouraging to know that, in any given congregation, God has provided every gift and talent needed to accomplish God's work there. The Apostle Paul reminded the church at Corinth of this truth: *Therefore you do not lack any spiritual gift as you eagerly wait for our Lord Jesus Christ to be revealed* (NIV, 1 Corinthians 1:7). Our responsibility is to discover our abilities, talents, and gifts – and then to get busy!

THE DEACON'S ROLE AS MINISTER

Because my father was a deacon, I (Keith) quickly learned how many things were expected of him. It wasn't just attending deacons' meetings and the various church responsibilities that took him away from home. There were phone calls, sometimes in the middle of the night, after which he accompanied the pastor to minister to someone in need. Unfortunately, the ministry-aspect of a deacon's role is often overlooked in many churches. The information in the following sections will provide the basic, common sense guidelines that you need to serve in a variety of ministry settings.

Ministry in Hospital Situations

There are special skills necessary for making an effective hospital visit.

Here are some tips:

1. Keep The Visit Short.
Remember – people are hospital patients because something is wrong! They are not going to be feeling their best. A short visit will let them know you care; a long visit will  exhaust them. Your goal is to make the visit meaningful without being too long. One pastor always carried his jacket when he visited at the hospital. He placed it on a chair as soon as he entered the room. He then sat down to share with the patient. After about ten minutes, he stood up, got his jacket (this communicated that he was about to leave), and had a *short* prayer with the patient. Sometimes patients later commented that they were blessed by his meaningful visit. The visit was actually shorter than was perceived by the patient. Because the pastor focused every single moment of the visit on the patient and the patient's needs for care and prayer, the patient perceived that *condensed* time as being longer. Quality of the visit is always better than quantity.

2. No War Stories.
Patients do not need to hear how someone died from the same health problem that they now have! They don't need to hear about horrible treatments! This particular patient has his or her own battles to face. What *is* needed from the person who is visiting is encouragement and caring. Your ears (for listening) are your greatest tools!

3. No Food Or Water Without Permission.
Patients are sometimes on food or water restrictions. Usually, there is a sign on the door of the room. If the patient asks for water, and there is no sign of a water pitcher or cup in the room, it is entirely appropriate to ask a nurse. Should a patient ask you to assist them in walking, it is wise to ring for the nurse and let someone who is trained in patient safety perform this service. Any patient, at any time, may require attention from the nursing staff, so always be respectful, and offer to step out into the hallway.

4. Encourage, But Don't Advise.
No matter how much you may want to help someone, do not presume to know better than the doctors and nurses. If a patient says they are experiencing increased pain or other discomfort, simply inform the nursing staff of the patient's complaint. You are not

there to diagnose or suggest treatment – *you* are there to provide spiritual comfort. You are there to represent the presence of Christ to the person who is ill. You are there to give encouragement. Your focus should be on ways of sharing your faith that will bring hope to the patient.

5. Ministry To The Family.
It is important to be aware of the needs of the patient's family, also. The stress on families when a loved one is hospitalized is significant, and additional stress may come from multiple sources. There may be stress that is work-related. There may be financial hardship caused by travel, meal, and housing expenses. Establishing a relationship with the family will help you identify key stressors and possible avenues of assistance. Conversation and prayer take place in waiting areas and hallways as often as they do in patient rooms. God may have sent you primarily to encourage a family member. Your mission is to both patient and family.

6. Answer The Phone.
It can be very tiring for family members to answer continuous phone calls, relaying the same information repeatedly. If the family desires, you can answer the phone for them, and either hand the phone to the patient, or provide callers with accurate information. This is a great help to a family in need of a phone break.

7. Don't Make Promises You Can't Keep.
It is very easy to say "You'll beat this" or "You'll be better in no time" when the truth is that you don't know! Giving false hope is false ministry. It is important not to promise even a return visit if you are not sure you can keep your word.

8. Do Not Cause Anxiety.
Some hospital situations create higher anxiety levels than others. When patients are in surgery or intensive care, things can become very tense. Make sure you do not become a problem by exacerbating the patient's or family's anxiety. You should be a calming and peaceful presence during such high anxiety situations. You may suggest that a family member take a walk or go to the cafeteria for a snack; this can be a way to minimize or reduce stress. You can volunteer to sit with the patient while family members leave the room for a little while.

9. Be Mindful.
It is urgent that you be mindful of those around you – other families in the waiting room or patients in nearby beds or rooms, who may also need a listening ear and a prayer. Be sensitive to their circumstances. Be open to the Spirit's leading in ministry.

Many people struggle through difficult times with little or no awareness of what Christ can do for them. Some of your most effective ministry may even occur on the elevator!

When Surgery is Involved

Surgery is serious business, even though modern medicine and phenomenal advances in health care and treatment have made many surgeries less problematic. But any surgery is serious if you or your loved ones are having it! Patients and families facing surgery are experiencing a critical [time that] has the potential to bring radical change into their lives. Issues [that] surface at times like these include: struggles of faith and salvation; health care issues (rehabilitation or long-term care expenses); end of life issues (living will, funeral arrangements); financial issues (insurance, copays, medications, lack of resources, disability, etc.). Even the "simple surgeries" come with these issues, so be sensitive to the many possible avenues where assistance may be needed. Be sure to inform your pastor (or the hospital chaplain) of any needs that you believe they are better equipped to handle.

Surgery hours can be long. Complications may arise. If possible, it is good to stay with the family when you can. At other times, you can check on them by a phone call to let them know of your prayers and concern. You *can* pray with people over the phone, by the way. Simple gestures like these provide much-appreciated support.

Confidentiality is a major necessity. Individuals and their families may share personal information with you. Never – EVER – repeat it! You may be permitted to share certain information, but only with their clearly expressed permission. Do NOT assume you know their wishes; always ask.

MINISTRY TO THE BEREAVED

No words can fill death's void. When a loved one has died, the heart finds itself teetering on the edge of a black hole. Bereavement is a critical time of ministry need for families. God's love, given in the actions of a caring deacon, can bring a much-needed blessing to breaking hearts.

Here are some suggestions for effective ministry with the bereaved:

1. Presence
Presence is more profound than words. Just 'being there' always trumps whatever words you might try to share. Remember, you represent Christ and His presence when you minister to the family.

2. Acceptance
The family is in shock and/or denial when death invades their lives. People react differently. Be accepting and sensitive to their reactions and their feelings.

3. Privacy
There is a time to talk, and a time to be silent. Everyone needs time alone to deal with death. Even though families are not up to it after the death of a loved one, so many things have to be done in a very short period of time. It becomes an even greater burden if the family feels like they have to host or entertain everyone who pays a visit. Respect them by helping them guard their time for solitude and rest.

4. Meals
Providing meals for the family is a great way to minister. As a deacon, you may want to help make sure that the church provides meals to make this time easier for the family.

5. Love
A loving spirit is the most important gift you can share with a hurting family.

6. Jesus
The family needs Christ's comfort. Pray with the family, and remind them of Christ's presence with them. Be sensitive to family members who are not believers. Be open to opportunities to share your faith, but be discreet.

Ministry After the Funeral

Bereavement does not end at the funeral; neither does the ministry of a deacon to the bereaved family. The sting of death delivers its poison over the course of the following year, as the family walks through life without the presence of their loved one. There are significant needs and opportunities for ministry during this time. In order for such ministry to be effective, deacons must understand some of the issues and feelings that deeply affect the family.

1. Special Days

Making ministry contacts with the bereaved is especially needed during the Holidays, on special family dates or events (birthdays, anniversaries, graduations, etc.). A visit, a handwritten card, or a phone call at these special times can be a blessing to the bereaved.

2. Returning To Church

It is important to keep in mind some of the difficulties that families may have with returning to church. If the funeral was held at the church, mental images of the casket at the front of the church can be painful. Music during worship services often causes emotional responses, especially if a song was part of the funeral service. A family can be overwhelmed if too much attention centers on them, just as they can be deeply hurt by neglect. Sensitivity is the key.

3. The Grief Process

If you minister to the bereaved, you should have some understanding of their experience. There are five stages of grief that people experience in times of loss. The stages do not always occur in the order listed, nor does one stage have to be complete before the onset of another one. A grieving person may experience more than one stage at a time – or become stuck in one particular stage. There is no set amount of time per stage. Grief happens, and it is resolved by the person who is grieving. While there are stages everyone experiences, each one's experience is unique. If you want to become more knowledgeable about the stages of grief, one of the best resources is the author Elisabeth Kubler-Ross, who wrote the classic in the field, On Death and Dying.[12]

---

[12] Kubler-Ross and Kessler, On Grief and Grieving: Finding the Meaning of Grief through the Five Stages of Loss (Scribner: NY, 2005). Also see http://psychcentral.com/lib/the-5-stages-of-loss-and-grief/

The "stages of grief" are identified as:

a. Denial: difficulty accepting that the person is really gone and is not coming back.

b. Anger: which takes many forms. The family can experience anger at the deceased for leaving them alone. They may express anger and guilt for their own actions or failure to act. They may feel anger toward the illness that took the loved one, and may even lash out at doctors, other family members, or God.

c. Bargaining: sometimes a person will bargain with God or others by making promises to act a certain way or do something if God or others will only do what he/she wants.

d. Depression: tears, discouragement, fatigue and inability to perform normal activities are some of the ways that this stage is manifested.

e. Acceptance: the loss is accepted, along with its pain, and the bereaved begins learning to live a life that includes their loved one's absence.

Remember, every person goes through the grieving process at his or her own pace and in whatever order meets their needs. Consider inviting a professional who works in the field to your deacons' meeting or to your church to talk about dealing with grief and supporting those who are grieving.

4. Legal Matters
Some families may need guidance on probating the will or making other decisions. Your role may be to give wise council or to guide them to people who have the expertise that is needed. Again, confidentiality is essential in such areas of ministry.

5. Presence
Being there with your flock is the most important way to walk with them through the deep valleys.

THE MINISTRY OF ENCOURAGEMENT

Everyone needs to be loved and appreciated. We all need to feel worthwhile, needed, and accepted. We crave human approval and have a need to be respected. We all need to feel that we belong, and that it matters to others that we exist. Many suffer with low self-esteem, feelings of isolation, and alienation. Because of these basic human needs, every deacon should be engaged in the ministry of encouragement! And a good place to begin is with those in our church body. Even a card or a call, a smile and a handshake or hug can be what someone needs to make it through another difficult day.

List 3 people you could encourage this week. What can you do to encourage them?

1. _____
2. _____
3. _____

MINISTRY TO THE ELDERLY

Ministry to the elderly in your congregation and community is one of the most challenging, but most rewarding, opportunities of service. Do you know that God places a high value on the aged? He expects us to care for them! Unfortunately, many churches are not meeting the needs of our senior citizens. How can you and your church be more effective? Before we explore ministry tips, we need to understand certain factors that are all part of being a senior:

1. Recognize that aging is a normal part of life.
   We will all become elderly, unless we die first!

2. Face your own fear of aging.
   It may hinder effective ministry with this age-group.

3. Realize that basic human needs for love and self-worth do not change with age.
   Every person of every age has the basic need to be accepted, to be needed, and to feel worthwhile.

4. Be aware that the elderly face many losses.
   This increases their likelihood of experiencing depression and discouragement.
   Consider the losses associated with aging:
   a. Loss of physical health and strength
   b. Loss of mobility and independence

c. Loss or impairment of eyesight, hearing, etc.
   d. Loss of family and friends as they, too, grow older
   e. Loss of respect because they are old
   f. Loss of job, and feeling needed
   g. Loss of income, and increased risk of financial crises
   h. Loss of their home if they require nursing care, or must live with relatives

5. Many seniors have already accomplished many of their life goals,
so they may feel discouraged about their future and usefulness.

6. Seniors may have fears about the future.
Some face loneliness and financial uncertainty due to the loss of loved ones.

7. Most seniors have physical concerns of one kind or another.
Many become depressed due to life's circumstances or chemical changes within their bodies.

We must learn to minister effectively to our aging saints. We are happy for the opportunity to share these suggestions, but the deacons at your church need to brainstorm together to list your congregation's particular needs, and ways to meet them. Make sure you ask the *seniors* for their ideas for a great seniors' ministry!

Here are our suggestions:

1. For the active senior:
   a. Provide easy access to classes and worship services.
   b. Provide comfortable chairs for their use.
   c. Be sensitive to their need to keep warm.
   d. Provide large print hymnals and Bibles, literature and bulletins.
   e. Provide transportation when needed.
   f. Develop a Senior Care Ministry for tasks that have become a burden to them, such as mowing grass, changing light bulbs, and cleaning out gutters. Seriously consider a phone tree ministry to check in daily on those who live alone.
   g. Provide activities such as trips, Bible studies, Senior adult choir, etc. Provide space at church for fellowship and activities during the week.

2. For the shut-in senior:[13]
   a. Assign church members to serve as liaisons between shut-ins and the church and its resources.
   b. Have a daily calling service to check on those who live alone.
   c. Provide transportation to the doctor and to the grocery store when needed, or do the shopping for them.
   d. Visit and send cards to remember birthdays and holidays.
   e. Provide video or audio of worship services and Sunday School, or have someone go to their home to teach the lesson each week.
   f. Do yard and house chores for them. Establish a volunteer data base of those who are willing to help.
   g. Listen! They need conversation. And hug them, when appropriate. Loving, appropriate touch is needed by everyone.
   h. Be available to them for whatever need they may have.
   i. Visit those in nursing homes, weekly and on a regular schedule if possible. Their days and weeks will have more meaning if they can "plan" on your coming.
   j. Be creative. Think of other ways to help. Ask about their needs.

It would be impossible, of course, for the deacons to accomplish all of the ministry needs in a congregation. It is important to remember that church leaders should enlist and equip *all* church members for the work of the ministry!

Evaluation:

In what ways does your church currently meet the needs of the elderly?

In what ways is your church failing to meet the needs of the elderly?

What training could you offer to those who are willing to help with these ministries?

What has the Lord said to YOU about what *you* need to do?

---

[13] Alice Cullinan, Widow Ministry, amazon.com and bn.com

Developing a Servant's Heart

How many of your childhood friends took piano lessons? How many *had to* take piano lessons? The ones who are forced can usually learn the mechanics well enough to get by  – at least until they're old enough to rebel! However, a piano student whose heart is elsewhere will not play like the one whose heart is the music. It is the same with deacon ministry, or any other ministry for that matter. If someone has the heart and the determination, they can learn to minister well.

Is it possible for a person to develop a servant's heart? Some are innately compassionate, and ministering to people in need just seems to come naturally. What if you know you have been called by God, but you also know that you aren't the *compassionate type?* Is there any hope that you can develop a servant's heart? We believe so! In this section, we will look at the characteristics of the ministering heart and discuss how you can develop and/or improve your own service.

Describing the Servant's Heart

We are men and women who want to serve the Lord. Whenever our hearts are stirred by God's Spirit, serving Him becomes our desire. That is the birthing of a servant's heart. But our heart still has to grow and learn how to minister. It is a lifelong journey. Along the way, we want to be able to measure our growth, to make sure that we are progressing. As you consider the following list of some of the traits of a servant's heart, you may find that some describe you and some don't. The ones that you think you do not possess are places where you can focus your efforts for growth.

Rate yourself on the following traits.

The individual with a servant's heart:	Low		Medium		High
1. is ready and willing to meet the needs that arise.	1	2	3	4	5
2. has no ulterior motives for serving, such as popularity, power, ego, need to be needed, sense of obligation, or assuaging guilt for past failures.	1	2	3	4	5
3. does not have to be persuaded to do the needed task.	1	2	3	4	5
4. expects neither reward nor returned favors.	1	2	3	4	5
5. serves because it is the right thing to do.	1	2	3	4	5
6. serves out of gratitude to God.	1	2	3	4	5
7. serves in response to God's love and in obedience to His command and call.	1	2	3	4	5

Evaluation: How are you doing? Where do you need to ask for God's help?

The Scriptures teach the necessity of growth in all areas of our lives, which includes servanthood. Don't be discouraged if you did not rate well on the evaluation scale. Developing a servant's heart is a lifelong journey. There is always room to learn and grow, even when your score is high.

The following comments and passages from the Bible are offered for your prayerful contemplation as you ask God to develop a servant's heart in you.

1. Our first commitment must be to spend time with the Greatest Servant of all, Jesus. He will change us into His likeness as we allow Him to do so.
   "The Son of Man did not come to be served but to serve" (Mt 20:28).

2. Having a servant's heart is not an option – it is an absolute necessity!
   "Whoever wants to become great among you must be your servant" (Mt 20:26).

3. We must learn to be attentive to the Lord's voice, and be a good student who listens with our heart.
   In Isaiah 6, the prophet Isaiah volunteered to serve when he heard the Lord speak.
   Eli advised Samuel to say, *"Speak, Lord, for your servant is listening" (1 Sam 3:10).*

4. Only *good* and *faithful* service will be commended by the Lord. Rewards for service that is pleasing to God are not withheld until we reach Heaven. At times we will hear the Lord's *"Well done, good and faithful servant"* now *(Mt 5:21).*

5. It is imperative to keep watch over our attitudes, disposition and behavior. Philippians 2 reminds us that our attitude should be the same as Jesus' when He left heaven to come to earth. And Paul reminds Timothy of the same principle:
   "The Lord's servant must not quarrel; instead he must be kind to everyone, able to teach, not resentful" (2 Tim 2:24).

6. We must serve wholeheartedly, and remember Whom we are serving.

    At the end of the age, Jesus will separate the sheep from the goats – according to how well we have served others (Mt 25).

    Paul reminded the believers in Ephesus of the same truth.

    Serve wholeheartedly, as if you were serving the Lord, not men (Eph 6:7).

7. All of the different ways to serve are important. Discover your gifts and talents, and use them.

    There are different kinds of service, but the same Lord (1 Cor 12:5).

8. By all means, guard against burnout! Service that has become a burdensome job will drain us, but service that proceeds from a full heart will invigorate us.

    Never be lacking in zeal, but keep your spiritual fervor, serving the Lord (Rom 12:11).

9. Never forget WHY you serve.

    Whatever you do, work at it with all your heart, as working for the Lord, and not for men (Col 3:23).

10. Ask the Lord to work in your heart to make you the servant that He wants you to be. Selfishness, not servanthood, is the default setting of the old nature. Let your constant prayer be, "Make me a servant, Lord."

As you read these suggestions, how did God speak to you? Do you know where to focus for growth? It will be helpful for you to share your experience with another deacon, for accountability and support. Pray for the deacons with whom you serve, that each of you will have a true servant's heart. Nothing is quite as disheartening as seeing people going through the motions of ministry without the heart for it!

Chapter 10

Managing Organizational Tasks

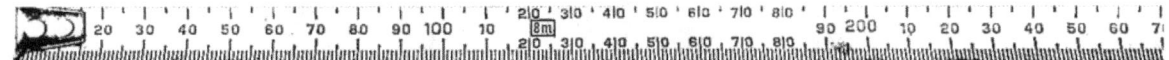

We all need practical help to grow in our walk with Christ. For that matter, anyone in any kind of ministry needs practical help to fulfill the call to serve God, and deacons are no exception! Typically, deacons are charged with the responsibility of ensuring that the church is equipped to function administratively, and protecting its membership and its assets. Unfortunately, a lot of churches have their heads in the proverbial sand, believing they are exempt from the same challenges facing other groups in the community. We must not become a casualty of this kind of thinking! Many outside forces that threaten a church's welfare were not problems until recent years. These days, having the proper documents in place to protect the church is urgent. Failure here could mean the end – closing the doors – of your church.

The suggestions that follow will not provide for every detail of your church's needs, but they are a very good place to begin. Producing and putting guidelines and protections into place will require a good deal of time for research, thought, and discussion. Various detailed resources are available to guide you as you build upon each of the suggestions made here.

Policies & Procedures

Constitution and Bylaws

An up-to-date constitution and bylaws are must-have documents for every church. Some think that such documents hinder the church and its ministry. While this may be true in certain instances, the purpose is to help the church operate efficiently. In many cases, churches never utilize these documents until there is a problem, which is when they may find them to be inadequate or outdated.

Some churches have followed unwritten guidelines for years without encountering a problem, but in a climate that encourages lawsuits, wisdom says "Be ready!" The saying "hindsight is 20-20" is true, but we need *foresight*. When we have to change our constitution in response to trouble that has already occurred, the church might be protected in future situations – but the damage has already been done! The church leadership should think about potentially problematic situations, and create a constitution and bylaws that will address contemporary issues. Of course, there should be provision for periodic reviews of the documents in order to *keep* them current.

What should you do if you see that your church is not operating according to its constitution and bylaws, or worse, it does not have these documents in place? If your church isn't presently following these documents, it is unlikely they will see the need to do so in a time of crisis or transition. One important example is the use of *Robert's Rules of Order*, which provides order and direction for business sessions. If your constitution calls for its use, then the church leadership should follow it. Leadership that is unfamiliar with the use of the *Rules* invites confusion and potential conflict when divisive issues arise.

Incorporation of a church protects its members in case of a lawsuit. The process is relatively inexpensive, and can often be completed without an attorney. If your church is already incorporated, it was required to adopt bylaws, and those bylaws must be updated regularly, with revised copies being submitted to the appropriate state government officials according to their deadlines.

It is not uncommon for the incorporation of a church to be on the checklist of persons searching for a church home. When a couple came to talk with me (Keith) about joining the church where I pastored, this was an important issue for them. "We will not join a church that is not incorporated, due to the liability," they shared. I believe they were wise for asking. If your church has not yet taken this step, a consultation with someone trained in this area of the law is advisable. You might be surprised to learn just how important it is to provide this protection for your members.

Recently, two churches in our county found out that their constitutions and bylaws did not address the serious problems that they found themselves facing. One had no stated guidelines in their constitution to handle a very difficult personnel issue. The other church's constitution provided them no protection whatsoever from what amounted to a take-over by their pastor, in league with an outside church group. In fact, when concerned members turned to associational leaders for advice, and were advised to consult their constitution, they could not find the document! The creation and maintenance of adequate church documents should be given priority in the administration of your church.

Sound Financial Policies

Stories about churches that found themselves in conflict with the Internal Revenue Service usually amount to *horror stories*. Obviously, it is important for your church to ensure its compliance with IRS regulations and reporting. It may be as simple as preparing W-2's for employees, or sending out year-end statements and 1099's. You should also know the rules for housing allowances, how to report benefits correctly, what does and does not constitute a tax-deductible gift, and how owning rental property can affect the tax status of the church. Thankfully, there are competent tax preparers and denominational representatives who can help churches with the needed information. "We didn't know" is not an excuse that the tax authorities will accept. The penalty for failure to comply with withholding requirements is just the same for a church as it is for any other entity that retains employees – about $100,000! – as one of our local churches found out recently.

Needless to say, your church needs to adopt sound financial policies, which should be clearly communicated to the entire church body. People are more inclined to give when they know that church finances are handled appropriately. Financial policies should take into consideration things like:

- How is the offering counted?
- Who counts it?
- Are there at least two unrelated individuals to count and deposit the money?
- Are they bonded?
- When, how, and by whom is the money deposited in the bank?
- Do the counters compare the amounts recorded *on* the envelopes to the amounts *inside* the envelope?
- Are there appropriate checks and balances throughout the entire process?
- Where and by whom are the records of giving kept?
- Do members receive accurate financial statements on a regular basis?
- Are the books audited on a regular basis?
- Are outside auditors used?
- How are budget decisions made?

It is hard to believe the number of embezzlement cases involving churches, especially when simple procedures and wise checks and balances could prevent them.

In fact, *many* church problems could be avoided by the adoption of and adherence to sound financial policies. Such policies are put into place not only to protect those who handle the church's money, but to give contributors confidence that their tithes and offerings are being handled with the utmost integrity.

What would happen to the assets of the church if for some reason we had to close the doors? Specific procedures should be spelled out in the church's official documents to handle such a possibility. As a nonprofit institution, the church's assets must go to another nonprofit institution. Many churches decide to give their assets to a local or state entity within their denomination. Such agencies will either use those assets to start another church or to further its mission work.

None of us wants to think that our church might ever have to close its doors. But we are responsible to be good stewards of all that God has entrusted to us – and that includes making sure *God's* assets will continue to be used for Kingdom work.

Sound Insurance Policies

Recently, we learned about a church whose sanctuary was destroyed by fire. It was located very close to a main highway that had been widened, bringing the front steps very close to the road. Sensibly, the congregation wanted to rebuild the sanctuary fifty yards further away from the road. That was when they discovered that their insurance policy stated that the church had to be rebuilt on the exact footprint of the structure that had been destroyed.

Leaders need to know the exact wording of the church's insurance policies, and policies must be kept current. Having an independent third party examine your policies, and especially the fine print, could prove to be quite beneficial. You will also want to check the liability and disability segments of your policy to make sure they are adequate for current needs. Don't ever make the mistake of thinking (naively) that "surely no one would sue a church!"

Security Issues

Sanctuary means a *sacred place*, where holy things are kept. *Sanctuary* also means *haven* – a place of safety, for humans (such as political sanctuary), animals (like birds), and even plants. Churches have long been understood to be safe places, places immune to vandalism or violence. Sadly, we know this is no longer true. Violence, desecration, and murder have come to our sanctuaries. The majority of churches, however, still do not have well-designed safety measures in place. What can you do to ensure that your church remains a *sanctuary*?

Consider the following safety precautions:

1. Adopt a plan assigning people to patrol the parking lot while services are in session.

2. Lock all doors during your services. This includes outside entries as well doors to offices, storage rooms, and choir rooms. Recently, at a local church, someone walked into the preschool area during morning worship, and stole equipment. The doors to that area had been left unlocked, and no one was on guard. How many choir members have had their purse ransacked or stolen during the worship hour? One church in our association even had someone setting fires in the educational building while members were in the sanctuary.

3. Come up with a plan to follow if someone tries to cause harm to your congregation during the worship service. In my first church, where I (Alice) served as the Minister of

Music, a woman stood up during the sermon and started threatening the pastor with loud screams. Everyone just stood there, doing nothing, because there were no procedures in place for such contingencies! Imagine what could have happened, had she brought a gun with her.

4. Health crises do happen ... at churches ... on Sunday mornings! Would you know what to do if someone became suddenly ill, fainted, or fell? Are any of your church members medical professionals? Do you know who they are? Have you provided training in the use of the Heimlich maneuver in case someone chokes? Does anyone know CPR? Who is designated to call 911 in the event of an emergency? Keep in mind that, even if you are blessed to have members who are medical professionals, you still need a plan. Your local law enforcement, fire, and rescue personnel are available to help you train your members. We should certainly pray that such untimely events never happen, but it they should, you will be ever so grateful that you were prepared to deal with them!

5. Protect your children and youth. In this culture, everyone knows that sexual abuse happens, and it happens too easily and too frequently. If your church does not have policies in place to protect youth and children, as well as procedures for reporting and handling all allegations of inappropriate behavior, you should be frightfully alarmed! You would be horrified to know how many incidents of abuse happen in churches. Don't be afraid of hurting someone's feelings by requiring background checks. This one procedure might protect some innocent victim from devastating abuse.

Church Mergers

Church leaders should know about new trends that have emerged recently. Some churches have been targeted for take-over by another group. We have seen these take-overs carried out in three ways: (1) a group of disgruntled persons left their church and joined a smaller one. A few months later, this new group voted the pastor out, and called the preacher they wanted; (2) a couple joined a church with the intention to influence the congregation to separate from its denomination; (3) a large church that wanted to expand by adding multiple campuses set out to find a struggling church so they could work behind the scenes to acquire its properties.

Churches *should* join hearts and hands to reach their communities for Christ, of course, and sometimes struggling churches *would* benefit from a merger. What every church *needs* to do is consider how it would handle any such unwanted attempts to take over or otherwise change its direction.

STAFF: CALLING AND EXIT STRATEGIES

When pastoral or other staff positions become vacant, the church's anxiety level skyrockets. At such times, there are many decisions to be made – some quickly. This will be especially problematic if guidelines for making those decisions are either vague or non-existent. The deacons of the church are usually involved in each stage of the decision-making process. The congregation will be less anxious if they are informed about that process. How your church leadership answers the following questions can help you plan calling and exit strategies, preparing your church for situations that arise.

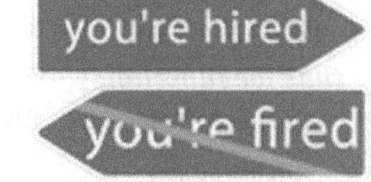

What considerations should be determined before the need arises?
1. Who secures an interim pastor or staff member? How is this done?
2. Who secures a person to fill the ministry position until an interim is in place?
3. How is the search team nominated and elected?
4. Will the search team continue after a person is called, and operate as a support team for twelve months after the new ministry leader is called?
5. What is the search process? How is a candidate introduced to the congregation?
6. What percentage of votes will determine if a person is called?
7. What background checks of candidates should be performed?
8. What are the *un*written expectations that a new ministry leader should understand?
9. What is the process for a grievance from the congregation or from a staff member?
10. What are the responsibilities of the Personnel Team, deacons, and other leaders in times of staff transition in the church?
11. How are decisions made about staff responsibilities, job descriptions, salaries, and raises?
12. Are there written policies regarding holidays, vacations, sick days, etc.?

These are sample questions to help you start developing your plans if you do not already have them in place. Sometimes a church's documents include information about the process of calling a pastor or staff member, but little, if anything, on the process of resignation. (What is the procedure for a minister or staff member to resign from your church? How many weeks' notice should be given? What is the policy about severance pay in a forced termination?) Proper documentation and well-designed procedures can alleviate stress during difficult times of transition.

WORKING WITH STAFF, LEADERS, AND COMMITTEES

The following conversation is often heard in churches: "I serve on a committee. We have spent months praying and working on this certain issue. We finally came up with a proposal for the deacons, and it only took them five minutes to throw it out! They didn't even bother to hear us out!" You can imagine the reaction of those committee members following such an incident.

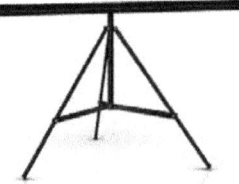
Does the way that we function as a church advance the Kingdom of God?

Deacons must listen to and appreciate the work of members and staff who also serve the church body. In a church that operates like the one just mentioned, you can expect to find committees that are ineffective and without vision. Members who once served with zeal now refuse to serve at all and will, in all likelihood, eventually leave the church. No one wants to be ignored or left feeling unappreciated.

Some pastors never meet with the deacons, and in some churches, the deacons don't meet regularly. There are even some churches that have not elected a new deacon in decades! Any situation you can imagine that includes churches and deacons is sure to have happened in some church, somewhere. Every church has a right to function as it pleases, of course, but there is one question that leaders should be required to answer: *Does the way that we function as a church advance the Kingdom of God in an effective way?* If deacons are not in conversation with staff or other leaders – if they are not planning, evaluating, and serving together – then the church will suffer. And the church will fail to reach people for Christ. We must learn how to work together, and do so with all of our might!

DEACON ELECTIONS

Deacon elections are critical times in the life of a church. The purpose of the election process is to discover and elect the most biblically qualified persons in the church to serve Christ. How effective is your deacon election process?

Consider these questions:

1. Is the number of deacons to be elected proportionate to the number of members?
2. How many votes does a person need in order to be elected?
3. Do you have a process for hearing the testimonies of potential deacons?
4. How long does one have to be a member of the church before serving?
5. Are expectations of service explained to the candidates?
6. Do you explain the ethics of serving (including confidentiality, faithful attendance at meetings and services, spiritual growth, etc.)?
7. Do you have a process (in writing) for replacing a deacon who cannot fulfill a term?
8. Do you have a procedure in place to guide all deacons, and to train the new deacons?

Some churches elect deacons based entirely on attendance. Recently, a pastor told us that each year the husband of one of his members is nominated. This nominee was neither a professing Christian nor a church member! Because he attended regularly, those who nominated him were unaware of his ineligibility.

A member of one of the churches that I (Keith) pastored let me know that he wanted to be elected as a deacon. He asked me what it took to get noticed and elected. I told him the best thing he could do was not to desire the position! My advice to him was to continue to serve Christ faithfully, and to leave it to God and the congregation to view his service and consider a nomination at some point. He did so and was eventually elected to the deacon board. Servants make the best deacons. Do you elect *servants* in your church – or people who just want to be noticed? The church is a spiritual body in need of spiritual leaders!

Deacon Family Ministry

Many churches have some kind of family ministry plan, indicating the intent that deacons should minister in a planned and positive way to church families. Usually in such a program, the deacon body or the staff divides church families into groups and assigns those groups to deacons. In theory, this sounds like an effective plan for ministry. Sometimes, however, the ministry never gets past compiling the list of names!

Why does this happen?
Here are some possible reasons:
1. There are too many people on the list for one deacon to serve.
2. There is little or no communication with the families.
3. Communications become confused when there is a deacon/family rotation.
4. Deacons fail to get to know the ministry needs of their families.
5. Ministry is often limited to hospital visits and funerals.
6. Lack of understanding of the expectations.
7. Lack of training for ministry in different situations.
8. Lack of knowledge of the deacons' spiritual gifts.
9. Lack of communication about who needs a visit.
10. There are too many families for each deacon to serve.

While this particular ministry model has a number of drawbacks, it *is* important that deacons understand their role as servants and ministers to the congregation. They *must not* simply function as a board of directors, financial managers, or consultants for problem solving.

It is wonderful when a family ministry plan succeeds. The care of families is not just the responsibility of the pastor and other staff. Deacons can minister to families through personal visits, phone calls, cards, etc. There is a need for ministry that is based on the gifts and talents of each deacon, of course. For example, it is important to realize that a deacon who faints at the sight of blood should probably not be asked to go to the hospital. If deacons discover what they do best, their ministry will be successful and rewarding. Each deacon should spend time seeking to know what God wants to accomplish through him or her during times of ministry to families.

Consider these possibilities for developing an effective ministry to church families:

1. Utilize deacons who have rotated off the board and are considered inactive.
This will lower the number of families for which each deacon is responsible, and allows for continuity between deacons and their assigned families. Having a smaller number of families will enable a deacon to be more supportive and responsive to the needs of his or her families.

2. The membership role is a great ministry tool.
You should study the resident and non-resident membership rolls, as there may be people on the inactive list who have needs that your deacons can meet. You can also contact inactive members to ask why they are absent from their church. There may be misunderstandings that you can help clear up. There may be family or health issues that caused them to drop out of church. If they are not planning to return, you can encourage them to worship at another church.

3. Ask deacons to select 1 or 2 *non*-deacons to help them minister to their families.
Deacons are not the *only* servants in the church!

4. Make it a practice for each deacon to have some kind of get-together for his/her families so they can become acquainted with others in their group.
Make sure each deacon communicates with every family, regularly. Birthday and Christmas cards let families know that they are on your mind. Put them on your prayer list. Reach out to them at church. Let them know you are available.

5. Deacons should have no more than ten families assigned to them.
If you do not have a sufficient number of deacons to minister to your entire church membership, you should ask others to assume this ministry responsibility.

6. Regularly publish a list of deacon family assignments.
With such a list available, any member can inform a deacon of a need they have or discover. Make sure addresses, phone numbers, and email addresses of deacons are readily available to their assigned families.

Church members are often only contacted when it's time for a new pictorial directory, or during a capital campaign to raise money. How meaningful it will be to them if they are contacted and told of your desire to get to know them better. We encourage you to work at this type of ministry in your church. Do not let the old adage "out of sight, out of mind" be true of you! Perhaps the most important chair in your Sunday School class or the church pew is the empty one. Someone should be filling it. Where are they? Find out and minister to them.

DEACONS' MEETINGS

Another important aspect of deacon ministry involves your meetings. Time and place, as well as the way the meeting is conducted, can determine whether or not your ministry is effective. Yes, everyone is busy, but as leaders of the church, your time together is vitally important to what God wants to do in and through your church.

Consider these questions:

1. Are meetings too hurried? Are they too long?
2. Are meetings characterized by open, frank discussion, or dominated by only a few?
3. Is every deacon respected and his/her participation encouraged and valued?
4. Do you have an agenda that guides the discussion?
5. How are the Chair, Vice Chair, and other officers elected? What kind of prayer and thought goes into this decision? Are there job descriptions for these positions?
6. Is there a spiritual part to the meeting other than opening and closing prayers?
7. How are decisions proposed and approved? Do you keep records of the minutes of your meetings? Who has access to the minutes?
8. How does the deacon body report to the church? Are reports printed and kept on file in the church?
9. Are all staff members allowed to share openly with the deacon leadership?
10. To whom does your deacon fellowship turn for help or advice when needed?

In my work as an associational missionary, I (Keith) met with many deacons from different churches. Some of those meetings lasted more than two hours, and accomplished little. At other times, the meetings were just an hour long, but were very productive. Some deacons met primarily for spiritual purposes, such as prayer and seeking God's direction about their church. Other meetings seemed to have no spiritual meaning at all, and were conducted like a board meeting whose sole purpose was to handle the business of the church. Do your deacons' meetings need to add that important spiritual dimension? Your church will be able to tell the difference.

DEACON ETHICS

At the close of a training event that I (Keith) led, a woman approached me and shared her appreciation for the conference material. While we talked, she shared her concern that leaders, especially deacons, understand the importance of confidentiality. Her church had faced several crises in the past years when deacons discussed sensitive issues with other people in the congregation. I told her that any deacon who cannot adhere to a strict policy of confidentiality should not serve. Deacons are privy to extremely sensitive information, which has the potential to hurt persons in the congregation. Some information is so sensitive that a deacon should not even share it with their spouse. Uncompromising confidentiality is a serious commitment.

Another important commitment that deacons should make is faithfulness – first to Christ, and then to the church. Some deacons never attend a deacons' meeting – not even one, during their entire term. There are even some who do not attend church services regularly. Are these leaders being honest with themselves if they are not doing their part to support the church? A deacon should want to be a genuine disciple – a servant, not simply an advisor. A deacon's service to the church should be a priority. God expects us to serve His flock. The church members who elect deacons know whether they are faithful or not.

For over thirty years, I (Alice) worked with university students. Teaching in the Department of Religious Studies, I had many students in my classes who were studying for the ministry. Regularly I engaged in private and personal talks with them as they sought my counsel. Unfortunately, I heard my share of stories of abuse at the hands of fathers who were church deacons. One I will never forget. This young man's father was a deacon who was involved not only in pornography but in wife-swapping parties with other deacons and their wives! Is it any wonder that his church was not reaching people for Christ in that community?

If there are behaviors in your life that do not measure up to God's standard of holiness for believers, there must be repentance. This is necessary, not only because you are blocking God's blessings to your church, but also because this makes you more likely to be the next one to fall! It is urgent that you deal with any temptation to sin *before* you succumb, causing the church to lose respect for both you and the office of the deacon-servant. You absolutely *must* live by the highest ethical standards!

The Bottom Line

Many of the situations mentioned in this chapter have the potential to disrupt the fellowship of your church body and ruin its effectiveness. Perhaps you have already dealt with issues that could have been avoided had our recommendations been implemented. When fellowship is disrupted, your church will not be able to fulfill God's plan. That is one reason why *unity* is so important.

An associational Director of Missions that I (Keith) know was filling the pulpit and helping a congregation work through issues surrounding a serious conflict that had resulted in the recent termination of their pastor. Addressing the negative atmosphere at the church, he shared the following with the congregation:

With the state this church is in today, you may as well hang the gospel on the wall, because you are not going to do anything with it for at least a year. Maybe a year and a half. You're going to be so consumed with taking care of yourselves and trying to convince the community that you're really not a fighting church, that you will completely forget Jesus' order to reach out to the world. You won't allow the Gospel to do anyone any good because you'll be too consumed with yourselves!

That was a strong and pointed message for that congregation! Remember that conflict and discord can do a great deal of damage to a congregation. Effective leaders know how to navigate the landmines and keep the church focused on doing the will of God. You are vital in making sure your church allows Christ to be Lord of your church. When you follow Jesus faithfully, your congregation is more likely to do so.

Chapter 11

Handling Church Conflict

Similar headlines fill our newspapers on a daily basis. An uncontrolled fire can quickly become a raging fury. Although fire is a part of life, we cannot appreciate the victims' suffering unless we have experienced it ourselves.

Here are more examples of headlines we see all too often: *"Treasurer Arrested for Stealing Church Money"* ... *"Pastor Jailed for Soliciting Gay Sex"* ... *"Youth Minister Convicted on Child Molestation Charges"* ... .

Here, however, are some headlines that don't make the papers: *"Worship Wars Splitting Churches in Record Numbers"* ... *"Power Struggle Undermines Church's Mission"* ... *"Apathy Closes Church Doors Forever"* ... .

How did you react to any of those headlines? How did you feel about the ones that probably won't make the papers? All of the headlines have a similar theme, however: something that should not occur *does* occur, and the result is devastating.

When you agreed to serve as a deacon in your church, the possibility of having to deal with serious problems in the church may never have occurred to you. Most of us would prefer to think of ourselves as *ministers* and not *referees;* as *encouragers* and not *arbitrators.* We were called to *lead,* not break up fights – weren't we? But, since we are all human, it is important to recognize that there will be conflict, even in churches. And *you* as a leader will be called upon to deal with it.

While we have no choice about whether conflict happens, we *can* choose to be prepared for it. Or – we can choose to avoid it, sweep it under the rug, or pretend it's really not happening. Sooner or later, however, reality will come crashing in upon that fantasy, and when it does, you will find that a small kitchen fire has destroyed the whole apartment complex!

We hope you will choose to be prepared, to address problems in a constructive and timely manner. "Remember, only *you* can prevent forest fires!" Most of us, however, are not trained in problem-solving or conflict management. That is why we have devoted an entire chapter to this one topic.

What About Your Church?

What problem areas have you observed in your church? List at least three problem situations that were discussed in some of your recent deacons' meetings. (Just list the topic, not the people involved or what was decided.)

Have you dealt with complaints from church members? What were they? (Topic only.)

In the last year, what were the top 3 conflicts the deacons had to address? (Topic only.)

Describe one or two strategies that your deacon body found to be helpful for handling problems.

WHAT IS CONFLICT?

What constitutes a conflict? *Conflict* occurs when there is a *difference, plus tension (Webster's Dictionary)*. The word implies tension between the parties involved, not just a disagreement or difference of opinion. Keep this in mind, because it is possible to have a difference of opinion that does not escalate into conflict.

There are some important facts to remember regarding church conflict. *Conflict is a dispute between two or more persons over values, goals, processes (the way things are done), and/or facts.* Problems occur when we try to force people to see our point of view or to agree with us. Unfortunately, it rarely crosses our minds that we can agree to disagree and remain agreeable. When a decision must be made about something that involves differences of opinions, goals, or processes, disputes can easily escalate into conflict. What is the basic issue in conflict situations? The answer may be simpler than you realize: your old nature and mine disagree. My "self" is upset because you will not do what I know should be done. As "king/queen of the hill," I insist that everyone listens to me. I am right and you are wrong. If anyone does not readily agree with me, I will gather people around me who *do*.

Is conflict *always* a problem between our old natures? Again, the answer seems obvious: those who are filled and led and empowered by the Holy Spirit don't experience such conflict. (For a review of the old nature, see Chapter 2.)

The Problem of Conflict

It is important for us to understand the underlying cause of conflict. The soul is the old nature; the spirit is the new nature, which is indwelt by the Holy Spirit. EVERY day (and *all* day), we make choices that determine WHICH NATURE rules our life – the *old* or the *new*. The OLD NATURE's goal: to be king of our own life. The NEW NATURE's goal: to allow Jesus to be King of our life. This fight is a DAILY one. It is fiercer than any ultimate fighting match you will ever see on TV! The battle WITHIN me is what complicates my relationship with YOU and the battle you are having within yourself. The result is conflict between us, because our old natures are too much in control. What can we do?

The following guidelines will help.
1. Realize that disagreements and conflicts are inevitable, because we are still human.
2. Learn how to spot the differences between the two natures so that you can deal with the fleshly nature before it escalates into a conflict with someone else.
3. Keep in mind that there are differences in our personalities, and in what we place value. Information fosters inspiration and diminishes conflict. Understanding our own personality traits and those of others will help us a great deal. (Review Chapter Five: personality types.) A refusal to try to see something from another's perspective not only causes conflict, it also *complicates* conflict.

What Else Complicates/Causes Conflict?
1. Self-centeredness (I don't *want* to see *your* perspective, because only *mine* matters).
2. Spiritual immaturity (I *like* operating out of the flesh).
3. Since I can't control things at home or at work, I will try to control things at church.
4. If you reject my idea, you are rejecting me.
5. If you can't see what I am saying, then you are wrong.
6. Leftover baggage from the past – issues from my own life that have impacted me.
7. Interpersonal conflicts outside the church (at home, at work, etc.).
8. Unwillingness to forgive those who hurt or offend me.
9. Low self-esteem.
10. Lack of problem-solving skills.
11. Fear of change.
12. Fear of confrontation, disagreement, or hurting someone's feelings.

Actually, there are *so many* factors that cause and complicate conflicts, that we have to wonder: **Is there anything that we can do to prevent its occurrence or to solve it when it happens?**

Strategies for Handling Conflicts

Before we look at strategies for handling conflict, let's look at two significant words: *rest* **and** *resolution.* Webster's dictionary gives the definition of *rest* as p*eace of mind or spirit.* There are a number of passages in the Bible that help us understand it. Here are the words of Jesus, recorded in Mt 11:28-29:

> *"Come to Me, all you who labor and are heavy laden, and I will give you rest. Take My yoke upon you and learn from Me, for I am gentle and lowly in heart, and you will find rest for your souls. For My yoke is easy and My burden is light."*

Many of us are familiar with this passage. We are drawn to it in times of turmoil and conflict, because those are the very times when we are not experiencing rest or peace of mind and spirit.

Webster says *resolution* means *to resolve something; to find an answer to; to deal with successfully; to clear up.* Unfortunately, this is the strategy we often miss. Both words are important, because without *resolution*, there will be no *rest!*

Weddings are joyful times that include the ceremony and festivities. Some years ago, I (Keith) was invited to officiate at a friend's wedding. During one of our pre-marital counseling sessions, the bride-to-be shared some of her deeply felt personal concerns. There were difficulties that had challenged her for many years, and she wanted help in finding answers and resolution. She confided that she had never really believed in God, but was curious. She remarked, "From what I've found out about Him, I think I need Him!" I shared with her how she could know the Lord personally, and after a time of sharing, she invited the Lord into her life to be her Savior. The major key to resolving her life issues and finding rest for her soul was belief in Jesus, and this belief gave her the peace of God for which she had been searching.

In order for any of us to be able to deal with conflict, we must start with what and Whom we believe. What we believe will decide whether we bring our conflicts to the Master, or sweep them back under the rug repeatedly.

At the beginning of this chapter, you were asked to list some of the problem areas in your church. At one of our deacon training events, we asked participants to write down and discuss issues that were either causing conflict or had the potential to do so in their church. What follows is their list of issues mentioned. Some of them may match your own list.

Common Church Conflict Situations:

Leaders not faithful in attendance	Budget issues
Church discipline problems	Choosing staff
Having the right people in right positions	Finances
Relationship conflicts	Issues over buildings
Traditions and ownership issues	Personality conflicts
Different opinions on music styles	Issues with change
Youth ministry	Heating and cooling issues
Theological differences	Repairs/Remodeling
Not enough willing workers	Different worship styles
Unity and setting priorities	Close-mindedness
Service too long or too short	Designated funds
Roles/Responsibilities of staff and other personnel	Gossip
Cliques	Jealousy
Support for missions	Failure to compromise
Leadership issues	Competition for control
Inter-generational differences	Transportation
Relocation issues	Staff differences
Use of facilities	Scheduling conflicts
Lack of initiative	Racial conflicts
Socio-economic differences	Fear
Hurt feelings	

Do any of these problems plague your church? Have you and the other deacons and staff attempted to resolve the issues involved? How successful have you been? Does the leadership in your church tend to pray and plan, or do they tend to avoid issues? As you think about circumstances that either *are* causing or *could* cause conflict, what strategies come to mind that will help you address and work through your problem areas?

Consider some of the following good and bad strategies for handling church conflicts.

Bad Strategies for Handling Conflicts

There are certain procedures for handling conflict that we should *avoid*. Note the following, and add any that you have learned from your own experience.

1. Ignore the problem, and hope it will go away.

2. Try to solve the problem without actually analyzing it first.
   Failure to assess an actual problem often causes more problems. A poorly analyzed problem or issue will often lead to a poorly developed solution.

3. Leave people in the dark.
   The failure to inform people often leads them to make their own assessments, which are usually based on hearsay. Always be discreet about what you share publicly, of course, but some things are best brought into the light for all to see.

4. Don't talk to the parties involved.

5. Do not consult the Scriptures, and do not pray for guidance about handling an issue.

6. Change the constitution or bylaws in order to settle the conflict.
   While conflict may reveal where change is needed, this is *not* a wise approach.

Good Strategies for Handling Conflicts

The best strategy for handling conflicts is to embrace Biblical values, and try to understand what the Scriptures teach about conducting business. Biblical values should be at the forefront of all teaching, preaching, worshipping, and service. Secular society faithfully teaches *its* values. Shouldn't we?

1. Decisions that the church makes must be based on Biblical values, not majority opinion. Whatever issues are causing the conflict should be thoroughly discussed, and prayerfully placed before God for His wisdom and guidance.

2. We must be as objective as possible in identifying the real issues.
   Ask yourself what might be some of the underlying motives among those directly involved in the conflict. Also be sure to search your own heart and motives.

3. We must seek genuine and complete resolution, refusing to settle for appeasement.
   Doing something simply to get by for the time being is rarely helpful.

4. We should seek outside help from those who are trained in conflict resolution.
   They will bring objectivity to the issue and may be able to see what you cannot. Your church's conflict will not hurt their feelings or threaten their self-esteem.

In your search for a Biblical perspective on resolving conflict, include these passages:

Jesus' prayer for His disciples:

> "I pray not only for these, but also for those who believe in Me through their message. May they all be one, as You, Father, are in Me and I am in You. May they also be one in us, so the world may believe You sent Me" (Jn 17:20:21).

Jesus' instruction to love one another:
By this all men will know that you are my disciples, if you love one another (Jn 13:35).
It is difficult for unbelievers to accept our message if we are exhibiting conflict with each other instead of love! The fallout from conflict is more important than winning an argument or getting our way. What's at stake may be the eternal destiny of unbelievers, and the effectiveness of the ministry of the church. The world observes Christians closely, hoping our message is one they can believe. This is why it is so important to live in harmony with our fellow believers, even when we disagree. Learning to resolve our disagreements in a Christ-like manner is absolutely crucial to our Christ-given mission. When we succeed, it is a witness for Christ. Whether we like it or not, when we fail, our witness is tarnished.

Conflict: Lessons from Life

When one of my (Keith) sons was in middle school, an assignment that he had was to complete a science project. After searching diligently, he chose a project that required only a few items: a six-ounce glass coke bottle, vinegar, baking soda, and a cork. The goal of the experiment was to measure how high the cork flew when the bottle was two-thirds full of vinegar and a spoonful of baking soda, and then capped with the cork. Since we already had the ingredients in the house, we tried the experiment. We didn't realize how much force was building up in the bottle. The cork blew out of the bottle and hit the ceiling so hard, it made a hole in it. We then decided it was best to take the experiment outside, where we repeated it to see how high the cork would go without a ceiling in its way!

There are some spiritual truths we can learn from this simple illustration. If you put baking soda and vinegar in a bottle and cork it, the matter is not *if* the cork will blow, but *when* it will blow. That is also what happens when we avoid dealing with church conflicts. The hurt feelings and anger may lie dormant for awhile, but the issues will continue to brew. And sooner or later, there will be a major explosion. Leaving issues unresolved is not harmless. It is really a way to add fuel to a fire. The longer we ignore conflicts, the greater the potential for a volatile upheaval.

You may be familiar with an airline crash some years ago that has come to be known as the "Miracle on the Hudson." The event made headlines across the country and especially in the Charlotte area, since the plane was headed from New York to  Charlotte. As the drama unfolded, we heard that the pilots had done a masterful job of flying that day, saving many lives. Think, for a moment, about that accident. Do you recall what caused the plane to go down? Take-off was normal. During the ascent, the plane encountered a flock of birds. When the birds flew into the jet's engines, they lost power. The pilot immediately sought help from the air traffic controllers. Realizing that he could not make it back to LaGuardia, or to any other airport, he began looking for a place to land the plane. There are few open areas in New York City where an airliner can safely land. The pilot realized that the Hudson River was his only option, and he would have to maneuver a perfect landing for the passengers and crew to survive. Captain Chesley Sullenberger – "Sully" – did land the plane, and every passenger and crewmember survived. That was indeed a miracle on the Hudson River that day, because the pilot assessed the issue properly and handled it appropriately.

In the wake of that near-disaster, experts began to consider ways to deal with the problem of birds near airports. How are we, God's church experts, designing ways to prevent church conflict, and ways to handle it when it comes? Are you and the other leaders in your church willing to take the time and make the effort to learn successful conflict management?

Have you seen the popular reality TV show called Undercover Boss? The program unfolds in this way: a company's CEO disguises her/himself, and then applies for a job in several of his own company's stores or facilities. Because he is disguised as a new employee, his own employees are charged with training him to do a job, to assess his potential. CEO's learn a great deal when they experience new employee training. They also learn what the other employees think about the company, and see for themselves the working conditions and the interactions between management, employees, and the public. Naturally, the disguised CEO learns some of the details about his employees' lives and the struggles they face. These experiences help him/her see the company from an entirely different perspective. Most report that their lives were changed when they were challenged to live up to the values and standards upon which the company was founded. They realized first-hand that real lives were being affected by decisions that the company management made. They learned a significant lesson: any major changes in the company had to start with the leadership of the CEO.

How does Undercover Boss relate to church conflict? When you and the other leaders in your church begin to deal with conflicts and how they affect people, you are likely to learn as much about yourself as you do about the problem situations. I (Keith) witnessed this very thing as I walked with a pastor through a difficult situation in his ministry. He had been terminated twice. Naturally, he felt dejected, and questioned his calling and ability. During a two-day period of assessment under my leadership, he and his wife completed personality and career assessments, and wrote fairly extensive personal histories. In our discussions, the topic of church deacons came up. There had been a deacon at each of the two churches with whom this pastor had collided. He believed that these conflicts were the reasons for the terminations.

Around mid-morning on the second day of our sessions, the pastor had an *"ah-ha!"* moment. Our discussion about his own personality traits, the dynamics of the conflicts in the two churches, and his handling of those conflicts had helped him see the problem. Stopping mid-sentence, he told his wife and me, "I just realized something! I think I know why this deacon and I could never get along – we are just alike!" It was as if a bolt of lightning had crashed close enough to light up the whole room. It was a life changing and a ministry-changing moment for that pastor.

Had this pastor not taken the time to examine his own personality, his background, and the conflicts that he had experienced in the two churches, I believe the very same scenario would have continued to play out in other churches where he served. When you are willing to confront conflict and engage in serious self-examination, you will become a more effective leader who can guide the flock safely through the storms that will inevitably come.

How the Early Church Handled Conflict

It is always best to be prepared, so that you will know what steps to take when conflict erupts. You cannot know all of the possible problems, of course, but you can be well versed in the basic principles of conflict management. Let's start with a look at how the early church handled conflict.

The early church certainly had its share of problems. For some reason, many of us have painted an idealistic picture in our minds of what it was like back then. But all we have to do is read Paul's letters to the early churches to see that they struggled with many of the same issues we face today! Let's take a few minutes to refresh our memories. We will look at the issues, how the leadership handled them, and basic principle(s) to learn to help us in our role as conflict managers. Regarding Bible references, we recommend that you read the *entire* Bible passage for greater detail about each situation. Also consider discussing the issues and their resolution as a part of your deacons' meetings – before you face a conflict.

Acts 5 and 1 Corinthians 5

The issues we see in these chapters are: *lying; deceit; incest*. These are quite serious issues that still surface today. Ananias and Sapphira were caught in deceit and lying. There were members of the Corinthian church who were involved in incest. How did the leadership deal with these difficult problems? Peter confronted Ananias and his wife Sapphira, pointing out their sin. Paul wrote to the church at Corinth, dealing harshly with their issue. What principle can we learn from these two examples? **The more serious the issue, the more severely it must be dealt with.** Are there guidelines in your church constitution and by-laws that will assist you in such serious circumstances? *Don't* wait until something happens before you make a plan!

Acts 15

A *difference of opinion* is a pretty common issue for churches. "If you have twenty people gathered," someone quipped, "you can be sure you'll have at least 25 different opinions!" Although this might be a humorous way to look at ourselves, it is certainly true that we are *all* very opinionated! And we *all* know we are right! The early church had the same problem. There was sharp theological debate about the Gentiles: some believed Gentiles had to become (circumcised) Jews before they could become Christians; others objected vehemently to what they believed to be nonsense. How did the leadership handle the problem? They sent representatives to Jerusalem, the church's headquarters, to seek a decision from the apostles and elders there. Note that they were willing to accept the leadership's recommended solution. There is an important principle here: **sometimes we need help from outside, from those who are more objective and more knowledgeable.** We ought to be willing to take advice, especially when we have asked for it!

Acts 6

No one can serve in church leadership very long before realizing that *complaining* is a major and a common issue. Most of the time, complaints focus on petty issues or minor differences of opinion, all of which have the potential to escalate into major conflict. Is this a new phenomenon? The early church suffered from complaining, too. Do you recall the reason for the first deacon election? Refresh your memory by reading about it in Acts 6. Some had complained that one group of widows was favored over another in the distribution of bread. How did the leadership handle the problem? Leaders were selected to take charge of this vital ministry, freeing the apostles to use their time for prayer and the ministry of the Word.

The result? The first deacons! It is unfortunate that the diaconate in many churches has morphed into something that looks more like a board of directors rather than a group of servants called to help support the pastor in the work of ministering to the flock and the community. **There are two principles to learn here: (1) deacons must get back to their main purpose – ministry; and, (2) we need to train people in the discovery and use of their spiritual gifts so that they will be effective in ministry.** If everyone understood and used his or her spiritual gifts and talents, many problems would be alleviated.

Acts 9

Another common (though less obvious) problem in many congregations is that of *preconceived notions* about *how things ought to be done*. Let's face it; most churches have some long-standing traditions that are simply not relevant today. This is *not* a discussion about Biblical truth or doctrinal standards; it is about our traditional ways and preferences for *doing church*. After Saul came to know the Lord, he wanted to be in fellowship with other believers, but they did not know whether to trust him. Some were skeptical; others welcomed him. How did the leadership handle the problem? Barnabas befriended Saul (now Paul) and then convinced the others to welcome the former persecutor into the fold. **The principle is that we must be willing to hear other believers who are more knowledgeable about the situation at hand.** It is counterproductive to have your mind made up before you have all the facts.

Galatians 2

Some differences of opinion, however, *do* border on doctrinal issues. Obviously, there are differences of opinion about what the Bible teaches. Divorce and women in ministry were two such controversial issues with which the early church also struggled. Peter and Paul, two key leaders of the early church, disagreed about whether Jews and Gentiles should eat together. Paul confronted Peter because Peter acted one way among the Jews and another way in their absence. Paul learned of Peter's hypocrisy and responded by confronting him in the presence of those who had been influenced by his hypocritical behavior. What can we learn from this situation? **There are two principles: (1) there will always be conflict over the Bible and what it means; and, (2) conflict among leaders is also inevitable, though the congregation is not always aware.**

Acts 15

This passage relates the story of another dispute that occurred between leaders of the early church. This one, however, could not be hidden from the congregation. The argument between Paul and Barnabas over John Mark's involvement in their mission was quite heated. The young man had defected on the first trip; Paul did not want him along for the second trip. Barnabas, however, disagreed. The mission team split. Sometimes differences among leaders cannot be resolved. Paul and Barnabas reconciled, but only after they had taken their separate ways for a while. What does this story of conflict and resolution teach us? **There are two principles: (1) sometimes there are no workable solutions and we must make the best of the situation; and (2) separation does not have to be permanent.** A difference of opinion does *not* mean that someone is wrong! Both parties can be right without the relationship being harmed. In Paul and Barnabas' story, the difference of opinion that led them to go their separate ways resulted in the expansion of the gospel.

Acts 8

In the church at Corinth, there arose another conflict having to do with doctrinal differences of opinion. There was conflict about the issue of whether it was acceptable to eat meat offered to idols, whether it was right to celebrate certain special days, etc. Some believed it was fine to eat the meat; others saw it as heinous. Both sides could support their positions. How did the leadership handle the problem? Paul emphasized the putting aside of personal bias and the importance of not causing others to stumble in their faith. If we find ourselves embroiled in such controversy, **our concern should be to avoid hurting another's faith.** At least, that is the mature way to deal with problems. Such differences become even more complicated when one side or both sides want to have their own way. Does the phrase *power struggle* ring any bells for you? Maybe it causes unpleasant feelings and memories to surface. This particular issue, unfortunately, comes with being human and living with other humans. Cain and Able had a strong difference of opinion about what was acceptable to offer to God, and Cain's anger led him to kill his brother.

3 John 9

We all like to be noticed and to feel significant, an often irresistible temptation for the old nature. This is a subtle piece of the problem in 3 John 9 ... *"Diotrephes, who loves to have the preeminence among them, does not receive us."* Isn't it interesting that John even called the man by name, and it was recorded in the Bible? The leadership certainly  didn't sweep this one under the rug. Diotrephes still gets noticed today – for his love of preeminence. Perhaps he got his wish. John also reported that Diotrephes used malicious words to accuse him, and even put some fellow believers out of the church. Talk about a power struggle…and this was in the early church! John dealt with it directly, though; he didn't pretend there was no problem. What we need to learn here is this: **it is foolish to sweep problems under the rug.** Our desire that they will disappear is not going to make them go away! Secrets usually shouldn't be kept. It is best to bring everything out into the light of truth. If a problem can be resolved privately, of course, that is always best. The key word is *resolved*, because failing to deal with issues causes them to escalate, to the detriment of the entire church body.

It is safe to say that the early church had just as many problems as today's churches have. Jealousy, cliques, quarreling, taking believers to court, improper behavior during the Lord's supper, copying spiritual gifts, differences about the legitimacy of tongue speaking, false teachers, confusion about the second coming of Jesus, grumbling, stewardship issues…and these are not all of the early church's difficulties! How did they handle so many situations? They taught and preached the truth about the issues, and called people to accountability. So must we.

BASIC PRINCIPLES ABOUT CONFLICT RESOLUTION

There may be a few people who thrive on conflict, but most of us probably want to eliminate it as quickly and painlessly as possible. And most of us would like to prevent conflict and its escalation whenever possible. Church leaders can find themselves on the brink of quitting when conflict seems unresolvable. A few basic principles to keep in mind will help us *before* we face conflict as well as *when* we find ourselves in the middle of it.

1. There will always be conflicts in a church because it is made up of sinful, selfish human beings like us! Don't worry about *why* you have the problem(s). Prayerfully focus on what needs to be done to deal with it, and how to help prevent it from happening again.

2. As much as possible, and with prayerful wisdom, leaders should keep things out in the light by involving those who need to know and are part of the solution. It will take godly insight to know with whom issues should be shared. Some people are better off not knowing. On the other hand, secrets are a breeding ground for resentment and misunderstanding, so be wise in your decisions.

3. Leaders must deal with issues as quickly as possible, before they have time to escalate. Many leaders think that a problem will resolve itself if they just wait long enough. Waiting may mean that the problem has more time to fester and erupt.

4. Have a plan! Know in advance how you will deal with various kinds of conflict, should they occur. Make sure your church's constitution and by-laws are both in place and effective for dealing with controversy (review Chapter 10). If you wait until you find yourself in the middle of conflict before you have a plan, you have waited too long.

5. Conflicts are best dealt with by spiritually and emotionally mature people. Make the commitment to be a maturing Christian who leads others to do the same. Your role as a deacon means that people have confidence in your spiritual perspective. Don't disappoint them.

6. Make prayer a top priority. Don't try to solve problems on your own. God knows the best way to handle any given situation. He is the One who can change hearts and minds. Go to Him and listen for His guidance.

7. Follow Scriptural guidelines regarding the problems you face. If the situation is not specifically addressed in the Bible, utilize biblical principles.

8. Keep your members informed and involved in church decisions. Don't make people have to wonder and guess, because they will usually arrive at a wrong conclusion – and almost always react badly.

9. People who are not united in a common mission eventually disagree. Your mission statement should clearly communicate your goals as well as the methods for accomplishing them. Make sure your church has a clear mission, knows its mission, and follows it.

10. Resolve to be part of the solution and not part of the problem in your church. There is nothing quite as sad as deacons who are the source of conflict instead of the ones keeping the peace.

The church is the Body of Christ. He expects us to work to keep it healthy. Diligence with regard to church health can keep problems to a minimum. Prevention is always easier than cure, of course. When leaders and members concentrate on spiritual maturity (living under the control of the Holy Spirit), and recognize the power of the flesh in each of us, conflicts will be avoided or quickly and successfully resolved.

Conclusion

"Look what I found, Alice!" My great nephew, who was seven, had been rummaging in the hall closet while I was catching my breath from a morning of babysitting. "It's a kite! Can we go outside and fly it?"

He was thrilled with his discovery, of course. I wondered if I could divert him from this particular adventure, as I had no energy left at the moment to teach kite-flying. I was greatly relieved when I glanced out the window and saw that there was not enough wind to hoist a kite. When I told him that, however, he opened the door to go out anyway, saying as he exited the house, "I can get it to fly." He headed for the backyard as I walked over to the window to watch. He was already halfway across the yard, the kite trailing behind him waist-high as he ran. Back and forth across the yard he ran, as fast as his chubby little legs would let him. He kept running back and forth, as he pulled the kite by its string, while it flopped against his leg. As He ran, he would glance behind him to see how high the kite had soared. The kite bobbed up and down waist high, alternately hitting him and the ground. I wanted to laugh, but felt guilty doing so. In one way, I hoped the wind would become strong enough for him to be successful for at least a few minutes. I wondered how many times he would make the trip across the yard before he gave up.

Six turned out to be the magic number of trips before he came back inside. Before I could compliment him for his effort, he grinned with excitement and said at the top of his voice, "I got it to fly, Alice! I got it to fly!" I tried to share his enthusiasm without laughing. When he headed down the hallway toward the closet to put the kite away, I said to him, "I guess we should wait for the wind." The words had barely escaped my lips when I sensed a gentle whisper in my spirit: "Alice, you are often just like that – so determined to serve me that you take off running with all of your might without waiting for the wind of My Spirit."

What a powerful message that I often still forget: it is too easy to try to serve God and minister to others in human strength. We forget Jesus' command to His disciples: "Tarry until you are endued with power from on high." This is the message we all need to remember and heed. We must have His power to minister and to live life to its fullest.

We have written this book to help God's servants accept His challenge to be the Body of Christ, honoring and serving Him faithfully and productively. We hope you will always remember that successful service in God's kingdom is impossible without the empowerment of God's Spirit. It is our earnest prayer that these materials will assist you in your personal spiritual growth as well as in your leadership of God's people. We encourage you to always seek His guidance and empowerment as you serve, and never doubt that He will always give you the wisdom you need to be a blessing in your congregation and community. "Wait for and depend upon the wind of the Spirit" as you walk with and serve Him daily.

For additional copies of this book, go to lamplighters-ministries.org or to amazon.com, or email us at lamplightersministries@gmail.com.